# LEAD TO WIN

## Pioneering Powerful Performance.

Nigel J. Copsey

# Contents.

# Preface.

For many years I have had a passion. I firmly believe, and this has been confirmed during my decades of experience and observations as a manager and as a consultant, that people love producing fantastic results.

I also firmly believe companies (read: "managers at all levels") actively prevent people from doing so — unwittingly in most cases. This can so easily lead to lower performance and expensive staff turnover.

At the time of writing, the U.K. is going through another recession. It is of no comfort to know that much of the western world is also swimming in perilous waters. This time, however, it appears to be causing adverse effects in the eastern "tiger" economies also.

Such long and deep economic troughs place a great deal of strain on companies but, even without such events, our competitors, both old and newly emerging ones, are always seeking to create better value propositions that will steal away our market and our loyal customers.

Consider this: two companies may have similar assets, a similar marketplace, similar products — yet one may be doing extremely well while the other is struggling.

Why?

There can be many reasons but, underneath them all, there is one major factor that contributes very strongly to the situation — the people in the organisation. From those in the highest rungs to those in the lowest, people are likely to be a main contributor to success — or, unfortunately, to a downfall.

At the core of this is the lack of effective leadership — at any level. Those in leadership positions seem unaware of either what is possible or how to achieve it — or both. Added to this, some processes are generally misapplied, serving to make things worse rather than better.

Maybe, like me, you have witnessed teams who seem to make miracles happen. They put heart and soul into achieving such a result ... and thoroughly enjoy the challenge as well as the achievement. Look again at your organisation or your part of it. How many of your team(s) are great winners?

For the majority, the reply would be "not enough". This, sadly, is supported by statistics, which I touch upon in the Introduction.

It is therefore important — even crucial — to have winning teams driving the organisation with not only the passion but also the ability to increase competitiveness. We need to understand how to create winning teams.

The strength of being able to Lead To Win - Pioneering Powerful Performance becomes critical. A necessity, not just a "nice to have".

It is why this book has been written.

# Acknowledgements.

There are many people to thank and acknowledge for the part they played in causing or shaping this book. Quite a number are the untold authors whose works inspired and shaped my thinking over the course of years. Perhaps the most inspirational were Douglas McGregor, whose books brought a simple but powerful revelation to me, and Peter F. Drucker, especially in his now ancient film on motivation that implanted in my mind a straightforward and clear message.

One of the acknowledgements I want to make is in relation to Drucker's material. My thanks go to Bridget Lawlor of The Drucker Archives who so very kindly spent much time and effort in tracing the Drucker film I saw some 30 years ago. Thanks to her I am able to share one of Peter Drucker's insights that made such a strong impact upon my thinking.

Added to these individuals are the numerous managers with whom I have worked, both colleagues and clients. They have provided experience of live situations of so many kinds from which I have learnt so much. A mere handful of these managers taught me some very important and harsh lessons on how not to do things!

In terms of the book itself, I owe particular thanks to Raj Gupta who, some 30 years ago, was the first to suggest I combine my experience and learning with my hobby of writing.

Much later, Gary Hicks confirmed the strength of the approach I had decided to take for this volume: "... as I sit down at my new desk, what do I do from here?" He made a very valid argument that this was more relevant today than ever before because of the career changes that people now make.

My thanks go also to Simon Copsey, who created the front cover for the book.

# Introduction.

The idea of writing a book on management/leadership has been on my mind for a very long time.

Part of the reason for the long gestation is the nature of the beast because, to my mind, the workings of the real world of management and organisations are a tangled web of strings. If you tug one thread, it has an effect on many others and, if you pull that one thread quite hard, it tightens tangles into knots, making the whole even more difficult to undo. This made the structure and approach difficult to determine.

The delay has actually helped. Due to the new experiences and observations accumulated during this time, ideas have matured and not only undergone refining and improvement but also resulted in what I believe to be the most appropriate direction in which to focus this volume.

## People *And* Processes.

I have regularly observed "solutions" for people and/or process issues are often inadequate because they are focused on only one part of the problem. Such piecemeal approaches may temporarily "fix" that part but the overall issue remains because the other contributing factors have a habit of ensuring most, if not all, the efforts are rendered futile. What is really necessary is nothing less than an all-encompassing and holistic strategy that addresses the variety of causes.

This book therefore covers two aspects of leadership: the people and the processes. These are intertwined and we must therefore have an approach to the work that encompasses both. Books on leadership seem to focus on the people element, but do not seem to bring in how we can manage processes in a way that helps people be more successful.

There is talk on "aligning people to the objectives of the organisation" but, in practical terms, how can this be done — and in a manner that enhances success? It is not easy but all acknowledge it is critically important. There are certain key elements and processes that facilitate that alignment and, as I discovered, unearth an almost frightening amount of missed potential.

The essence of the book is therefore to be a practical guide, illustrated with live examples, to take any manager/leader, whether new to the role or more seasoned, from a simple "how can we start?" to the beginnings of "how we can continually increase momentum and results."

## *Would You Use A Formula 1 Car To Get The Groceries?*

Lead To Win - Pioneering Powerful Performance is an effort to get management at all levels — especially at the top — to understand and to realise the amount of potential that lies untapped inside their, or their part, of the organisation. So many organisations are like Formula 1 racing cars being used solely to toddle around to the local supermarket to get the family groceries. A definite quantum leap in performance is under the bonnet but is rarely, if ever, unleashed.

I do not use this simile lightly. People can and do achieve great things, amazing things, just because they want to. No doubt you have at least heard of the book "The Man Who Planted Trees" by Jean Giono. This is an allegorical tale but a true counterpart exists in real life, in India. Jadav Payeng single-handedly grew a sprawling forest on a 550-hectare sandbar in the middle of the Brahmaputra.

Another feat of human endeavour, again in India: a landless farmer, Dashrath Manjhi from Bihar, decided to end the difficulties faced by himself and his fellow villagers by doing the "impossible". By hand, he dug a 360-foot long, 16-foot wide, 25-foot deep cut through a high hill. The man-made one kilometre gorge cut the distance to the nearest town with medical and other facilities from around 50km to just 8km.

*(Information on the feats of both these individuals can be found on Wikipedia.)*

I am not suggesting individuals are likely to undertake such tremendous feats of perseverance and dedication in the workplace. Even so, when you witness significant performance growth many times, the reality of the hidden power is clear. In sales, an area where performance measurement is easier, an almost 50% increase in revenues from the same team is just one live example of the kind of thing to which I refer.

Just imagine this repeated across sales teams and replicated in most, if not all, other areas or departments of your company.

And it is possible to achieve.

There is further supporting evidence of the amount of potential just waiting to be unleashed.

Having undertaken hundreds of McQuaig System™[1] psychometric profiles in India, I decided to do a brief and rough analytical study of these and some interesting, although alarming, statistics arose.

Before we look at the figures from the study, we need to first understand the implications of morale levels. I would ask you to think back to a job you really enjoyed and at which you were successful. What was your level of performance? Did you produce excellent work? Did you really work — or was it actually too much fun to be classified as work?

Now think of a role you really disliked. It will potentially make your heart sink as you remember it. What was your performance like then? And was it work — or sheer drudgery?

In this latter situation, we tend to "just do a job" because we have to. Our mind is elsewhere — perhaps even planning an escape from the "prison" in which we have found ourselves. Performance is "just sufficing" at best and possibly quite low. We tend not to go the extra mile to achieve excellence in what we do. By contrast, in the role we enjoy, it is normally quite the opposite. We break down barriers and make things happen. We take things to a new level — and get a great deal of satisfaction from it all.

So just imagine: if you are running an organisation in which practically everyone is having great fun in producing fantastic results, what would happen to the business? (Think Google Inc., Apple Inc. and others of their ilk.)

Conversely, if practically everyone in your unit or organisation is unhappy and cannot wait to get away from the company, what levels of excellence are you likely to see?

Putting it more directly, what kinds of problems will the company be likely to face?

With this fresh in your mind, consider the statistics from the McQuaig profile review:

- Only 5% are really enjoying themselves.
- 24% are comfortable.
- 34% don't feel particularly good.

---

[1] The McQuaig System™ is a copyrighted psychometric tool set from The McQuaig Institute of Executive Development in Toronto, Canada.

- 37% are potentially fed up and looking to quit.

With a massive 71% who are less than comfortable, does this not speak volumes about hidden — or lost — potential?

Some people will say that the difference in performance is not measured here, so where is the link between it and morale level apart from the memory game we played about our own performance levels a moment ago?

The answer to this is the quantitative results I mentioned earlier and this book contains many live cases in order to better illustrate concepts and ideas in a "natural setting". A large proportion come from my own direct experiences for the simple reason that I experimented a great deal based on what I read and thought about when trying to be an effective leader/manager. I was forever working on converting the theories into real-life practice.

The only people who can Lead To Win are managers, those leading a team at any level in the organisation, whether they are the CEO, a Team Leader or a Supervisor. In other words, you.

The concepts will not only help you understand why so many companies face multiple internal "challenges" such as  lack of effective leadership, low engagement levels and staff attrition but also illustrate how these can be prevented. You are the only person who can make this real difference to your area of responsibility.

You will also see how you can not only remove, or at least lessen, these negatives but also how you can build strong positives in their place.

If you are the CEO, you can influence the entire organisation, which is likely to bring significant overall performance improvements.

Will you be the one to blaze the trail or will you wait for someone else to take the initiative — perhaps one of your competitors?

# The Structure of This Book.

The book is broken into three main parts:

## *Part 1. Getting Started.*

I have learnt from experience that trying to make the kind of dramatic change we seek to obtain involves a great number of things and, on first starting the process, one really does feel it has become a huge and inevitable tidal wave that is overtaking and overwhelming us. There is no "sink or swim", only "drown!"

The first section therefore starts the manager in the charting of a new course in "bite-sized" chunks rather than get lost in the flood of work that really needs to take place.

## *Part 2. Getting Deeper.*

Once the new direction has been established and the team has adapted to the new ways of doing things, we can now work on powering up the engines to "full steam ahead". This entails extending the concepts and building upon them, refining our outcomes.

## *Part 3. Summary, Conclusion And Bibliography.*

These give an overall summary, as well as additional reading for those who are interested in widening their knowledge.

# Part 1: Getting Started.

*SYNOPSIS:*

*Because so much untapped potential can come to the fore when starting this approach, it can be difficult to know where to start.*

-=-=-=-

With so many kinds of problem draining potential from a company, it is very difficult to know where to start. Should we tackle engagement first, or leadership? On the other hand, should we focus on stemming the severe haemorrhaging of staff or perhaps work on increasing productivity to become more competitive in the market?

Then there are processing problems: errors, late deliveries, partial deliveries, quality issues, cost overruns, machinery or other equipment failing, staff shortages, skill shortages. You can no doubt add a lot more to this list from your own experience.

And, if all that is not enough to cope with, there are what I term the "hidden" problems, where people have learnt to live with them "because they've always been there" and "there's nothing you can do about it." As a result, they aren't seen as problems any more but each is continuously acting as a handbrake to slacken momentum.

I know what it feels like. I have been there. I have had to face situations where the problems are so great and so many that not only is one at a loss on where to start, there is also that thought that creeps into one's head and whispers: "why bother? Why bash your head against a brick wall? Where will it get you?"

We need a systematic approach that will guide us through the maze. We also need the flexibility to apply appropriate parts of it to the most pressing priorities while dealing with the whole. Something that can be applied to just the area we ourselves are responsible for because we cannot necessarily influence the entire organisation from where we stand within it.

We will now set up the first stages in preparing to Lead To Win — Pioneering Powerful Performance.

# 1.0. Setting our Forward Focus.

*SYNOPSIS:*

*We cannot lead if we ourselves don't know where we should go. The company vision may not help because it is often difficult to relate it to our role.*

*To get our focus, we need to be able to understand the main elements of our work and its purpose. The recognisable and generic "categories" mentioned in this chapter will provide clarity of focus and direction for most companies and most individual teams within the company.*

.=.=.=.

The intention of this first phase of Pioneering Powerful Performance is to gain and give clarity in our direction. It is much easier for all of us if we not only know where we are going but also why we are going there. Another way of putting it is, how can we lead if we ourselves don't know where to go? Realising the wide range of problems we are likely to have, our approach is to now categorise everything into straightforward headings.

Although a company may well have some kind of vision and/or mission statement, it will potentially aim at creating great value for all the stakeholders in a balanced way, preferring none over the others. This aspect is very important as failure to do so can result in a low long-term performance.[1]

We need a method, a structure, for helping us avoid such negative situations and to provide a framework with which to work positively towards looking after all four sets of stakeholders.

The time I spent in Operations Development provided me such a structure. The concept I learnt there certainly brought clarity, especially for those who were not at the highest levels and therefore less able to see the big picture. It places the normal, everyday things we do into distinct categories that enable clarity and focus. These categories are:

- Budget (cost controls)

---

[1] John P. Kotter, James L. Heskett: "Corporate Culture and Performance": The Free Press (1992) ISBN: 0029184673

- Controls (e.g. Health & Safety rules, accounting rules, laws of the land, the monitoring of our standards)

- Quality of product/service

- Revenues (sales)

- Staff Morale

- Timeliness (of delivering products/services)

If we maintain high levels of performance in all of these and also keep them in balance they will, in effect, meet the demands of all our stakeholders and hopefully go further to "wow!" them.

It would be impractical to believe that things will fall neatly under one heading or the other. For example, let's assume we have a process that is slow and cumbersome and adversely affecting our delivery timing. We focus on this and streamline the process so it is quicker, more efficient and also effective. The probability is that, in increasing productivity, we have also affected the "Budget" heading in a positive way because we can more profitably utilise the time released from this process.

How, then should the project be classified? A simple but effective way of viewing it is as a timeliness issue. This is the main reason for tackling it. The fact that it has brought a cost saving of x hours a month is an added bonus to be recorded as achieved. To make things more interesting, a further benefit could be staff morale. This would be the case if the poor soul on our delivery counter had to keep trying to placate unhappy customers when s/he has no control over the process. That can most certainly be very demoralising. Is this all? No. Unhappy customers have the knack of deciding to find a supplier that will cause them less grief (and also advise everyone they know to do the same), so even the prevention of further lost revenues can be affected by the improvement.

It is important to quantify/qualify the improvements gained from an activity, particularly in an operations or back-room function, because whilst in the thick of things we begin to wonder if we have made any progress, made a difference, to our area of responsibility. There is always something demanding a fix, so we only see the problems rather than celebrate the successes. I have certainly experienced this, more than just a few times! Reviewing the achievements is a refreshing experience and brings back the positivity into our demeanour, I promise you.

There is another very important reason, as we will see a little later on.

# 1.1. An Overview Gives A Vision.

*SYNOPSIS:*

*It is often stated that we must create a compelling, exciting and down-to-earth vision for our area. Generally, it is considered by managers as either the responsibility of the Board and not applicable to them or they do not understand how to create one.*

*We look at how this can in fact be achieved — and in more than one way.*

-=-=-=-

When the word "vision" is used, most managers and employees will react by saying this is nothing to do with them. That is something the Board of Directors determines.

Yes, maybe so. Some Boards put together something very grand and think they have done their job and have a great belief that everyone will now follow it.

It doesn't often happen that way, though.

> After much discussion and thought, the directors of an organisation created a vision: that they would have a customer base of £1 million and a managed asset base of £1 billion. This was "translated" to a simple statement "Million - billion."
>
> To send this message to all employees, a special gala event was held one evening and a short presentation made. To help drive the message home, the event was covered in the house journal where the concept was briefly explained once more.
>
> When I was with the head of HR three or four months after the launch, he mentioned the simple, catchy and challenging vision was not getting anywhere. People did not seem to be excited by it in any way. What had gone wrong? Why weren't people as excited about the idea as the Board and senior management were?
>
> I asked what the statement was. "Million - billion" I was told.
>
> What does that mean, exactly?
>
> "We will increase our business to have a million customers with a billion pounds (sterling) turnover within five years."
>
> What is the average age of your staff?

"23-30"

When you were that age, what did a billion mean to you?

"The figure '1' with a lot of zeros after it. I'm not sure how many zeros, even now."

Apart from that aspect, how does the vision affect me as a member of staff in terms of the work I do each day?

"Er ...?"

How many of your managers are living and breathing this each day and translating the vision so I, as their direct report, can see how my work affects the vision?

"None"

Then please do not expect any changes. We first need to get the managers to understand how to translate this and then live it and breathe it. Then you will find things happening.

A vision can be very important. It can help create a great organisation — or a great department. We do not have to be a director in order to create a vision for our team.


We will now need to do some homework before moving forward.

Consider this: how many of us end up "just doing a job", making work seem almost meaningless at times? How can we turn it into something that makes us want to get to work on a Monday morning?

What most of us tend to either forget or not realise is the reason behind the work we are doing. Describing the role of the department or of a job in terms of "what we are here for" can be a real eye-opener for some. Are we just working on the Reception Desk or are we ensuring customers and visitors feel welcomed, see us as efficient and helpful, and walk out feeling positive about us as a company to deal with? Are we just working in Parts Department or are we ensuring we keep the right levels of stock to satisfy our customers' needs quickly and efficiently with a delicate balance that prevents the costs of overstocking?

What is the real purpose of our area? To what end are we working? How does what we do make a difference? To whom? Why?

This approach to our work can remove "meaningless" and replace it very strongly with "meaningful" or even "critical". We can see the importance of our actions and how they affect our customers, be they external or internal. We now have a good reason to do what we do and to do it well.

Let us now add another dimension to this.

Now we have greater clarity about our purpose, we are most likely to find it linking into our Key Results Areas (KRAs). Remember the Parts Department we just mentioned? That links clearly into timeliness and costs, for example.

With KRAs in mind, we need to take stock of the overall view of the situation in our area. What are some of the more important, perhaps generic, issues that need to be improved upon? Maybe our timeliness of delivery is a major challenge. The question is how can we help our team to focus on this more strongly and with great passion?

This is the kind of situation I found myself in:

> One of the departments for which I was made responsible comprised about 12 people. We faced regular Operational Audits every 2-3 years. On checking, I found the last audit had highlighted a lot of serious faults. On checking out what progress had been achieved in terms of rectifying these, I discovered absolutely nothing had been done, even though the audit had taken place about 18 months ago. This meant that within 6 months or so, there could be another audit and, if these issues remained unresolved, it would have severe implications for the Unit, the department ... and myself.
>
> Things had to change and, in spite of the terrible time constraints, change quickly. For this, it was crucial to have every individual in the department not only involved but very committed to the "cause".
>
> This prompted a "vision", which I started to communicate and act upon: inculcating the value in all staff in the department that "my desk will not let the department down in the next audit."
>
> Whenever work was presented for sign-off, I would ask the individual what an auditor would say about this paperwork, and why. Getting the expected answer of "I don't know", I would request the person to go through the Operations Manual regarding this part of the process. This generally had the desired effect of educating individuals about the procedural controls they should follow. Naturally, I also explain why this particular control existed and the potential negative consequences the company could face if it was not properly exercised.
>
> It was done in a positive manner and, I believe, due to taking time out to explain the "why", the controls began to visibly improve. People did take ownership of the vision — not a single

one of them wanted to let the department, his/her colleagues, down.

After 10 months, while I was on holiday, the audit team descended upon the Unit. I didn't know about it until my return, when I was suddenly greeted by everyone in the department crowding around me, shouting jubilantly "we did it! We did it! The auditors didn't find any faults — not even a single minor infringement!"

In effect, a vision had been created for the unit. It had been made into a positive challenge. It was something that people found important and relevant. No-one was castigated or blamed, instead time and effort went into fostering learning.

Sometimes, the opportunity may present itself, as happened to be on my next assignment.

This time I was posted as Manager in charge of a branch unit comprising about 95 people. I soon discovered that standards of work and of customer service left something to be desired. In fact, there was a great deal that needed to be put right but I was really puzzled over how this could ever be achieved.

Interestingly, the opportunity presented itself when I was reviewing some work with one of my supervisors and found a number of errors and omissions. On raising these with the supervisor, the response was: "well, what can you expect? Anyone who is useless is posted into this branch."

I knew from having worked in the same region a little earlier that this was potentially true — or at least was the general perception. It was potentially regarded as the worst performing branch. However, I decided to take exception to this. "I am in this branch. Are you saying I am useless?" I asked.

"No, sir!" exclaimed the supervisor suddenly realising the trouble he may now be in!

"Are you useless?"

"No sir. I don't think so."

"Well, I think we can be as good as any other branch in the region — if not better — and we are going to prove it," I stated with conviction.

That became the defining moment. The vision was set. This was the driving force behind the whole branch from then on. Interestingly, supervisors came to me to report information they had gleaned from their friends in other branches: time and again, we were becoming well ahead in completing certain large "projects" that had to be completed by all units each half-year.

On top of all this, productivity increased, profits were up, and customer service was improved. The people in the branch could now take pride in their work. They were not useless and their results spoke loudly for them.

It is now time to consider a vision for the area for which we are responsible. Can we sum it up in a short sentence? Something like a rallying call that makes people feel they want, they must, be a part of the action as an employee reporting to us.

It will give us questions to ask ourselves as we do things: "how will this prove to our suppliers (customers/staff/shareholders) we are ...?"; "How can we ensure our customers see us as ...?"; "Is there something else we can do that will ..."; "How will this affect our staff's vision of us as ..."

It becomes a part of our "vocabulary". On everyone's mind. On everyone's lips and, most importantly, in everyone's actions.

As their manager, we will need to live it, breathe it, eat it, dream it. We must make it fun and exciting, not just a mantra that is repeated over and over without thinking. Celebrate the successes as they happen.

## 1.2. Weaving the categories into the fabric of our work.

*SYNOPSIS:*

*How the "categories" can be used as Key Results Areas, enabling clarity of focus. How they can also provide a basis for action planning and monitoring in a positive and constructive manner.*

-=-=-=-

The next step is to build a system, a process, which helps us keep our focus on these categories. However, processes are all very well but why should anyone want to work with them? You can almost hear the kinds of response we might get when trying to introduce them: "Why not stick with what we do and know?", "What difference will it make anyway?", "How long will this fad last before it fades away in the shadow of a new one?"

Understandable sentiments. There is the temptation to view these as the "normal resistance to change."

From personal experience, I find people generally are not as resistant to change as we like to think they are. In fact, they will often be more than happy to grasp change — even drive it for themselves. Actually, this latter point is the key.

When we have change forced upon us for no apparent logical rhyme or reason, we are much more likely to resist. Let's face it, changes are not always explained adequately. We wonder whether we will be adversely affected, and this is exacerbated if there is lack of trust in our manager or in the management in general.

In contrast, if we are encouraged and supported in finding for ourselves new, quicker, easier ways of doing things, we are much more likely to drive our ideas to fruition and at the same time add value to the organisation. I have personally experienced this when managing people and have been pleasantly surprised by the thinking and the ideas that come forward.

> When managing an area of a large office, I had to change the role of a number of clerical staff because a change in systems meant their jobs would disappear. Being new to the branch, I did not

know much about the experience of these individuals, so called on the knowledge of their supervisors. One man was currently handwriting statements, copying the entries from the ledgers. I asked his supervisor what the man's experience was.

"Writing statements," came the reply.

"I know that is what he is doing now but what previous experience has he had?"

I got the same reply. Being new to India and my then broad Kentish accent was not helping my communications generally, I decided to try asking a different way. I asked how long the clerk had been working with us. The answer was 27 years' service to date.

"What was the job he did when he first joined the bank?" I then enquired.

"Writing statements."

"Are you telling me this fellow has been sitting on the mezzanine floor writing statements for twenty-seven years?"

"Yes."

As you can guess, I was now in a real fix. What do you do with a person who has potentially been turned into a cabbage by the workplace? I sought out a role that was going to be straightforward to learn: using a large machine with which one typed a customer's name and address onto metal plates that were then used to address envelopes.

He settled in fine. However, about a month later, he came to me with a request. "I have been talking to the mechanic who services the machine and he says that we can get an adjustable bracket that fits onto it to properly align different-sized envelopes. This will make it so much quicker and easier to print the envelopes neatly. At the moment, I have to try to do it manually, which is time-consuming. This bracket costs (the equivalent of £1 Sterling). Can I order one?"

A person who didn't "just do a job" but thought about it.

Now consider (as I did at that very moment) the amount of potential we had lost from this one person over the 27 years he had been working for us. Similarly, how much has he missed out on by not being given the opportunity to add value and grow within the organisation?

Where does all this fit with building a system?

If we create a system that helps individuals in what they want to achieve, they are more likely to welcome it and take it forward. It will take a lot of discipline and adjustments on our part but the rewards we get will be worth it. Not only that, it will add value to both individuals and to the company.

## Using these categories as Key Result Areas (KRAs)

Because the six categories we mentioned earlier relate to most, if not all, of the operations within an organisation, they form a very convenient set of KRAs upon which everyone can focus. It allows us to obtain a clearer picture as well as a convenient structure to analyse our overall results.

Obviously, not everyone will have responsibilities under all heads. For example, many operating departments may not have any direct inputs on revenue generation although, as we saw in the example in last chapter, they may have an indirect impact.

For some readers, the mention of KRAs may sound ominous because are these not part of an appraisal process? If so, it is likely to be a difficult concept for people to accept, mainly because appraisals are one of the most negative episodes in working life in a fairly large percentage of companies.

The answer to this is "yes" and "no".

## Contradictory?

No. The point is that, yes, it will be a part of the appraisal system but no, it need not be a negative experience. In fact, we can make it a highly motivational exercise if we do it in a positive manner, which is what we will be discussing in a short while.

If you have worked in at least one company, you will no doubt have faced an appraisal system. More than this, you will also be aware of how people feel about appraisals. Maybe you have been lucky and had/given positive and inspirational ones but, for most, it is a proverbial boil on the backside. Generally, we don't relish the idea of undertaking an appraisal, whether we have to run it or receive it. We postpone the assessment of our direct reports because we are "too busy" but the underlying reason is we would rather not be faced with the task.

We don't like passing judgement on others. It is not nice to tell someone they are not up to scratch and they need to improve. We might fear they may make things difficult for us, by withdrawing cooperation for example, if we give them a lower "score" than they want or expect. If we recommend a pay rise or a promotion and they don't get it, we also have to deal with the aftermath.

Besides, what difference do appraisals actually make? They are, surely, only carried out to enable HR Department to tick another of their boxes? It makes one wonder whether they should be dispensed with completely. It certainly would make life easier.

Or is there a way of making appraisals part of a process that stimulates, excites, motivates and brings high performance?

You bet there is!

It is from measuring their performance.

Let me immediately clarify. How would you feel if your manager in the course of your appraisal writes against your KRA results:

*"S/he overhauled the delivery process and achieved a 10 minute delivery time compared with the earlier 40 minutes. In doing this, s/he also achieved a cost saving of 25 hours a month, saved our counter clerk from having to deal with 2 complaints a day and due to this we have lost only one customer a month instead of the previous average of 5."*

... And does the same for all your other achievements?

Would you feel your inputs have been noticed? Your contributions recognised? Would you think the value you have added has been properly quantified? Would you see it as just and fair?

How would this affect how you view your manager? How is it likely to affect your attitude towards your work and the plans you would like to make for the coming months?

Now let me ask another question. How many managers do you know of that write these kinds of remarks in appraisals?

Now yet another, more important, one. When have you ever done it?

"Ah!" I hear. "That is all very well but what about the negatives? What about the goals they did not reach?"

Indeed, this is a critically important aspect that can make or break the appraisal experience and can either enhance or kill off Pioneering Powerful Performance. It fits more comfortably with something we will be discussing a little later so we will deal with it then.


*Kicking off the process.*


Getting the process started is the most difficult part because we are wading into a potentially muddled situation with lots of possible problems, both clear and hidden. To attempt to put them all on the table and start working with them is a colossal task and will likely cause confusion and consternation and, to add to this heady mixture, we are new to the concept and concerned about whether we are going to get it done right — or not.

It is easier and more productive to dip our toe in the water, become accustomed to the temperature, and then steadily immerse ourselves.

Before anything else, it will be essential to explain to our direct reports what we plan to do and why. And one part of this is to help them write their own appraisals — and to give them the opportunity and support to make these appraisals great ones!

So, what are our aims?

- To have a system that helps us focus on the key objectives of our company and "wows" our stakeholders;

- so we can ensure we align our work and results to these objectives;

- in a way that is logical, common sense, and practical for our level and our work;

- To help each of us plan what we want to achieve and how we want to achieve it;

- Using a simple but effective method of monitoring progress to ensure our plan is working the way we want it to;

- Or gives us a warning that we may need to re-think what we are doing or how we are doing it.

It is all to do with "Scoring Sixes".

# 1.3. Scoring Sixes.

*"If you want to plan for thirty years, plant trees; if you want to plan for hundred years plant men." ~ Jamsetji Nusserwanji Tata (who founded the Tata Group.)*

Our own results depend upon the results of our team. To obtain a significant and sustainable increase in performance, we have no option but to help improve the performance of each and every team member.

We therefore need to coach them in "Scoring Sixes" when they bat on behalf of the team. We must help them be more and more successful in what they do.

It may sound an enormous task, especially if they are not doing particularly well at the moment. I faced such a situation myself when I took over an area comprising well over 100 people and I could see so many gaps in so many aspects of the work that it was frightening. It was not the fault of the people in that office. They had not had much training nor received any effective management, so the situation was only to be expected. But it was my job to turn all this around — and quickly.

One of the most powerful ways of achieving this is "Leading From Behind."

### 1.3.1. Performance Management? No! Lead From Behind instead.

*"To lead people, walk behind them." ~ Lao Tzu*

*SYNOPSIS:*

*Motivational theory is difficult to put into practice and rarely has the desired effect.*

*"Leading from behind" is a simple concept that demands no more than honest commitment, self-discipline and careful practice on our part.*

*Yet it is effective in building morale, motivation and unlocking powerful performance.*

-=-=-=-

Lead from behind? Is this a typing error? Surely, leading means being firmly at the front and taking people forward?

It does sound contrarian but Leading From Behind is a powerful way of leading as well as an exhilarating one. As one manager I coached described his first experience with this method of leading: *"I must admit I have never felt so much inner satisfaction before ..."*

I find HR departments trying to install Performance Management systems but I view these the same way as the Appraisal Systems. They are a form-driven process and, generally, are ineffective. They are completed "for HR so they can tick another of their boxes".

Performance cannot be managed. Performance is something that you unlock. You set it free to fly high and soar like an eagle. Companies and their managers tend not to do this and I surmise there is a fear of losing control. Either that or a lack of understanding of how people behave.

Leading From Behind is the key that unlocks performance. It is one of the core components of Pioneering Powerful Performance. It takes a great deal of courage to change from being a "controller" to unlocking the power of performance. I have seen supposedly tough managers very hesitant to use this approach for fear of losing control over results — very negatively. When they actually succumb to reason and try it, they found they did lose control over results — very positively!

I worked with a small team of Regional Sales Managers to help them gain better results and stem attrition. When introducing the concept of Leading From Behind, they were visibly concerned. However, they did agree to give it a try because of the serious challenges they faced.

Just one month later, during a session to review progress, their results were:

*"A major improvement in performance which can be sustained. Staff have been relatively stable by comparison. A definite improvement in one-to-one skills and this has been reflected in a direct increase in overall results."*

## So, what is Leading From Behind?

It is a method of leading that I pieced together as a result of my studies while in an international management training centre and later refined from observation and experimentation.

Let me take you through a little of my experience that will also serve to illustrate some of the building blocks of my thought processes.

How do we get people to do things that need to be done? How do we motivate them? As a young manager, having had no management training, these were the kinds of questions rolling around in my head. I took a naive stance: what did my "bad" managers do that turned me off and what were the things the "good" ones did that really motivated me? It was a simple case of trying to avoid certain things and attempt to do others.

Except, to my consternation, it didn't work. For quite some time I could not understand why. It was very frustrating. Where do I get the answers? Later, it began to dawn on me that what motivated me did not necessarily motivate someone else. People are different and are driven by different things.

I was lucky in that I was soon assigned to a newly-established training centre and one of the new subjects on its agenda was supervisory skills. My predecessor had built a good course and I was inducted into running it. This began to open my eyes. However, one thing was lacking: practicality. I was learning and teaching motivational theory but how does one actually put it into action? How do I identify what drives a particular individual? How can I determine what a particular person needs?

I believe I have learnt much since then thanks to the experiences I have had. However, a few episodes along the way have definitely taught me a great deal.

One of these episodes occurred much later when I was looking for some interesting video material for a management course whilst in the international training centre. I reviewed a film on motivation by Peter F.

Drucker. He was meeting a Sales Director who asked how he could motivate his salespeople.

"Forget about motivation," said Drucker.

This floored me! How can I use this in a session on motivational theory? Surely motivation is one of the most important jobs a manager has to undertake?

"Assume that each of your salespeople wants to do the job he or she is being paid for and then it's your job as their manager to make sure that they can do the job they are being paid for," Drucker continued. "Remove obstacles to performance."

The Sales Manager replied: "Obstacles to performance? We don't deliberately place obstacles in people's way. At least I don't think we do."

"Have you ever sat down with your sales force and said to them what are the few things I as your manager and the company do that help you in doing the job and what are the four or five things we do that get in the way and hinder you?

"Nothing so damages and destroys the respect for a manager as his making it difficult for his people to do the job they are being paid for and then criticising them when they don't deliver." [2]

This was one great "Aha!" moment for me.

Because it is such a powerful concept, I have carried this as one of the important "tools" for helping managers who complain about lack of performance by a direct report. I ask them how many people want to fail. How many want to do a bad job?

The answer is always "hardly anyone."

I follow this with "so all we need to do as managers is to understand what is preventing them from performing the way they want to and help them remove the obstacles. Then they will automatically perform better."

Let me give a real-life example.

---

[2] *"The Manager And The Organization. Helping People Perform - What Managers Are Paid For"*, Peter Drucker. The Drucker Institute at Claremont Graduate University.

In our office, we had floor tiles of marble chips and, although the cleaners were working on it daily, it never seemed to sparkle. It always looked dirty. I called the Head Cleaner to the stairs, from where one could get a good view of the office floor. I said that I knew he and his team worked hard at cleaning but somehow the floor looked dull.

The man's immediate response was defensive: "but we clean it every day!"

I told him I had seen that and reiterated the fact that, for all their efforts, the floor did not sparkle. I asked if he had any ideas about what we could do.

"They stopped us from using a mixture of two cleansing powders and the scrubbing brushes," he replied. "They wanted to cut costs."

"Are you saying that the floors shined better when you used those?" I asked.

He confirmed this. I checked the pricing and, although the materials they used now were cheaper, the savings were not particularly significant. In fact they were quite small. I therefore gave the authority for them to have the right stuff and, in a matter of a few weeks, I was able to call the Head Cleaner back to the stairs to appreciate the results of his team's work: a bright new floor that they had created between them. He was justly proud.


Another inspiration for the Lead From Behind concept came from the "Aha!" moment I got from a saying I read long ago but unfortunately cannot remember nor trace the name of the person to whom I should attribute this:

"You can take a horse to water but you cannot make it drink — is a fallacy. All you have to do is make sure it is thirsty first."

Many people do have dreams. They do have aspirations. They do have passions about certain things. They may not want to rule the world but there is often something, however small or short-term, that they would like to achieve for themselves. Helping them to find a way to get there through work activities provides a perfect way to get them motivated. It is a powerful win-win situation.

This was reinforced by two brief, live examples of this concept in action.

A telephone sales manager told me he was concerned about the fact that one of his most successful people was beginning to "go off the boil" and her sales figures were beginning to fall. Staff turnover in sales does tend to be higher than in administration areas and his experience told him that the situation with this individual was a sure prelude to losing her.

"What is she passionate about? What are her interests?" I asked.

"Nothing to do with work, unfortunately," he replied. "She is a Francophile. She loves France and anything French. She is fluent in the language and brings French books and magazines into the office to read during her breaks. Her holidays are always in France. Why do you ask?"

"Have you asked her if there is any way in which she could bring her interest into her work?"

"No, of course not."

"Why not do so and see what happens."

The Sales Manager did ask her that question and he got an interested response. "I never thought of that!" she apparently answered. "I could make a point of calling French-owned companies over here in the UK and speak to their French senior managers in their own language. Not only would it be fun, I may get more sales that way!"

There was a slight pause before she continued: "but would that be allowed?"

"There is nothing to say you can't do it. So why don't you go ahead. It sounds good!"

Thereafter, her enthusiasm soared, her sales increased significantly and she did not move out of the company — at least not for quite a while.

The second striking example of this was with another Sales Manager's dilemma.

The National Sales Manager (NSM) of a publishing company was told by one of his Regional Sales Managers (RSM) that he was planning to find a new role. It seems he wanted to be promoted to the next level but this was not possible because that level was the NSM position.

The NSM requested my help. He said he accepted the reasons the RSM wanted to go and appreciated the fact the he had been open enough to give warning so he could look for a replacement. However, the RSM was so good, the he wanted to try to keep him longer, if that was at all possible.

I asked how much of the NSM role did the RSM have any experience to speak of? The reply was "hardly any".

"So he is looking for such a role elsewhere with little experience that will help him be a strong contender?"

"Yes."

"Then if it is not going to be a political problem with his peers, could you not start giving him some of your responsibilities in order to prepare him for his next step? He is a smart fellow and I am sure he will see the benefit of holding back to learn a lot more so he will have better chances when he does move."

The NSM agreed to try this and started the process. The RSM stayed on for another 10-12 months before landing a good role in another company.

There is an interesting post-script. Several years later, when he hit a ceiling in the company to which he had moved, he sought to come back to my clients at an even higher level and was successful in doing so.

The way I describe Leading From Behind when coaching or training managers is:

- To get behind the person and see where they are looking.
- Where they want to go. What they want to achieve.
- Then we can potentially help them find a way of getting there.
- They are then working hard for what they want.

The practicality of this has been demonstrated in the live examples we have just seen. It helps unlock their true potential to perform to let them soar as high as they can get.

You will note the words: "helps unlock". Although an important part of the process, there is more that needs to be done to take them all the way there. We will therefore cover these aspects also.

### 1.3.2. Commencing the KRA process.

*SYNOPSIS:*

*The likely outcome of this approach is revealing a great number of problem areas and opportunities, so much so that it can seem both confusing and difficult to move forward. There is just too much to tackle.*

*We need a simple, straightforward start that builds the team's confidence and abilities without it being perceived as threatening.*

-=-=-=-

The most thorough method of approaching the Key Results Areas is to dig into all aspects of the six KRA elements to determine what needs attention, prioritising, action planning, then moving ahead with the plans. However, as I discovered when I tried it, this unearths so much that needs doing — to the extent that one is buried in a mass of things and it becomes difficult to distinguish the wood from the trees.

It will also be very discouraging for the team, which is the last thing we need!

In spite of the thousands of things that might be ready to shout at us for attention, we need to find a way of focusing on only the most obvious. The first stage of getting our direct reports comfortable with this way of working is therefore to ask them to look at their own area of responsibility in terms of the six KRAs and think about whether there are certain aspects they think should be improved. We do not ask them to find something for each KRA that relates to them, merely to state what they think should be done better.

We ask them to prioritise the items that they have identified on the basis of which are the most critical and why. As we shall see in the later chapter on problem solving, another way of looking at it is "what, if put right, would bring the greatest contribution to your results?"

The next step is to request them to create a step-by-step action plan to tackle the top priority item, aiming at bringing the results in line with their expectations.

A sample format appears on the next page.

Figure 1: Sample Action Plan Format.

## ACTION PLAN

**Dept/Unit:** _____    **Position:** _____    **Name:** _____

**Date:** _____    **Plan Ref No:** _____    **Priority Level:** _____

**OBJECTIVES:**

**REASONS/BENEFITS:**                    **NOTES:**

| Step No. | Start Date: | ACTION STEP | By Whom | Target Date | % Complete |
|----------|-------------|-------------|---------|-------------|------------|
|          |             |             |         |             |            |
|          |             |             |         |             |            |
|          |             |             |         |             |            |
|          |             |             |         |             |            |
|          |             |             |         |             |            |

**Agreed By:** _____    **Agreed By:** _____

**RESULTS ACHIEVED:**

Depending on the amount of resources (e.g. people, time) required to complete the action plan, it may be feasible for the next highest priority item to be planned for as well. However it is very important not to allow them to fall into the trap of trying to deal with too much at a time as this might well stretch their resources to the point that nothing much gets done on any of the plans, which would obviously be counter-productive as well as stressful.

From the specimen action plan format, you will notice that, although target dates are mentioned, start dates are also called for. The reason for this is very practical. People are prone to diarising the target date and, on opening that page in the diary as it is reached, they then realise that they have a lot of work to do that should have been done earlier! Diarising the start date is a much more useful reminder.

When they have completed the action planning, particularly for the first time, we should set up a date and time for a meeting to discuss the plans they have made. This will enable us to ensure they have thought things through adequately and their plan appears to make sense. On top of this, they may need additional support in terms of resources or our input. For example we may need to obtain a specific authority for them to move ahead on certain parts. This will not only mean we should initial or sign their Action Plan Format to signify our agreement and commitment to their plan, but also that we will need to diarise accordingly to make sure we properly support their efforts to achieve stronger results.

This discussion is extremely important because it sets the "culture" that we need to build and, of course, this needs to be extremely positive. We will therefore take a look at a very crucial concept that will assist us in this process: "Ask! Don't tell!"

# 1.4. Building people's morale & performance using the "*Ask! Don't tell!*" concept.

*SYNOPSIS:*

*The "Ask! Don't tell!" concept is an extremely powerful support to enable us to "Lead from behind" in a positive and effective manner.*

*It is difficult to do because of our built-in habits, which we need to work hard at changing to ensure success in this venture.*

*Some live examples from differing situations illustrate its comparative strength and flexibility.*

-=.=.=-

This is an extremely simple concept but it is also an extremely powerful one. Yet it is one of the most difficult things to do because it means totally changing our past habits — I should know, because my natural leadership style is to tell people what to do!

Let me illustrate with a live example of how this works.

A General Manager of the I.T. function in one organisation was facing a very difficult problem. There was to be a substantial change in a crucial system and this required a strategy to be hammered out and also to have all the Department Heads committed to making it a success. Unfortunately, the GM was having difficulty in getting these very people to express opinions and ideas openly and he was certain their stated commitment was words rather than something actual and tangible.

The manager reported that he was finding only endorsement to his ideas. No-one was willing to criticise or put forward alternatives, even though he had requested them to do so on several occasions. As a result, he felt that he was getting neither the best possible solutions and ideas for the project nor the commitment from the team, yet both these facets were so very vital to the success of the whole system change.

Because of the importance of the project, he asked me to help him overcome this huge blockade.

On examining his approach to running his meetings, I discovered that he generally outlined the situation or problem that they were to address and, in order to get the ball rolling, placed an idea on the table for discussion. He then asked them to criticise the idea or to come up with alternatives that would achieve the result in a better way.

The result was, as he had mentioned, merely an endorsement of his idea.

"If your boss were to put before you his idea on solving a problem and asks you to criticise it, how would you feel about doing that?" I asked.

"Not too positive," came the response.

"Why?"

"Well, he is the boss after all. I am not sure he will take kindly to his ideas being rubbished."

"And yet you are asking your people to rubbish your ideas. How do you think they take to that?"

"When you put it that way, I suppose they feel the same way as I would."

"So we need to find a way of asking for people's ideas without making them feel vulnerable. We also need to elicit their ideas, rather than hybrids of our own. Would that be correct?"

"Yes."

"What is the best way of finding out what a person's ideas might be?"

"By asking them what ideas they have?" Then he frowned. "But I have been doing that."

"Or have you been too busy telling them your ideas ...?"

"I see what you mean. I should go into the meeting and just specify the problem and ask for their ideas?"

"How do you think they will react?"

"Well, some will possibly come out with ideas but some are very quiet and tend not to voice an opinion."

"Then we need something extra. Supposing we specify, well in advance, what the area of discussion will be and ask them to think it over in readiness for the meeting?"

"No problem in doing that."

"But supposing I say that you should not specify the problem itself?"

"How will they be able to think of solutions?"

"Solutions to what?"

"The problem, of course!"

"What problem?"

"The problem we need to discuss."

"So you feel you should define the problem?"

"Naturally. Unless I do that, they won't have anything on which to base their thinking."

"Who says that you have the definition of the problem correct?"

"What do you mean?"

"Have you ever found that some people see a problem from a totally different perspective to your own?"

"Yes."

"Sometimes that perspective gives a whole new identity to the situation?"

"Yes, that has certainly happened to me in the past occasionally."

"So why restrict people to the way that you perceive the problem? Why not let each individual see it from his or her angle. This will bring a broader analysis and a wider scope for manoeuvre, won't it?"

"Yes. I see your point. So in future, I should just give a subject or a fairly broad overview of what we need to look at, ask them to think through the problems that are involved and how they think these can be best tackled?"

"What do you think will be the reaction to that?"

"Each person will look at different aspects to the situation and we will have the whole thing analysed from a number of angles. Problems that I don't see will be identified by someone else. Solutions to various problems can be discussed by everyone to find the best approach. That sounds good."

He paused in thought. "Except for one thing."

"What is that?"

"Supposing they come up with ideas that won't work? ... Ah, but then I'll have my idea in reserve, won't I!"

"Who will judge whether their ideas will work or not?"

"The project is my responsibility, so I will have to do that."

"And what will be the possible reaction when you tell a person, or a group, that their idea is not good enough?"

"They'll have to think of another idea."

"You haven't answered my question. I'll put it another way. How do you feel when your boss tells you that a great idea you have thought of is useless?"

"Ah. I see what you mean. But how do I make sure that the solution ends up as one that will work? After all, the success of the project is vital."

"Do your team members want it to succeed too?"

"Yes, I think so. They are a loyal bunch of people."

"So, if you ask them to analyse the solution as a group, to see whether it will stand up to the test of practicality, what do you think their reaction is likely to be?"

"I reckon they will be happy to do that."

"So they can quite easily come to the conclusion that, for a specific reason, the idea won't work?"

"Yes."

"What will happen then?"

"They are likely to try to find another answer."

"Interesting, isn't it! But I would like to make another suggestion." I added.

"Which is?"

"Well, I have learnt from experience that I do not have the monopoly on good ideas, nor for that matter, on being right all the time."

"Therefore?"

"Well, in analysing the solution that may seem wrong to you, perhaps something will come out of it that shows you that it was an extremely good idea. It was just that you did not fully understand the full implications of their thinking at the time."

"Sounds fine to me. But there is one other point."

"What is that?"

"Well, I am supposed to be their manager, yet you are basically suggesting that I leave all the work and all the thinking and problem solving to them. Have I read you correctly?"

"You have certainly read me correctly. What is wrong with that?"

"How will they view me? They'll find me pretty useless as a manager, surely?"

"How do you feel if your boss allows you to approach a problem in your own way, takes you through an analysis that helps you to be certain in your own mind that your idea is sound. How do you feel if that same process helps you to realise that there is a flaw in your thinking and encourages you to find a way around that?"

"If only he would!"

I grinned. "QED?"

The final results were that this senior manager was not only successful at drawing his Department Heads out and getting ideas and commitment, he also persuaded them to follow a similar route with their respective teams, to cascade the involvement down through the entire IT function. The whole process of change went extremely smoothly and everyone had felt that they were always aligned on the best overall solution, having aired differences of opinion on many occasions along the way.

The fact that analysis of ideas was done with the objective of seeking the best possible solution had enabled people to criticise constructively and with a positive purpose and this ensured that criticisms were not taken as personally as they might otherwise have been.

"Ask! Don't tell!" is powerful and extremely useful. However, it is crucial to ask questions that seek information and that cannot be perceived as a judgement of the individual or their ideas. The way I describe this to people is as follows:

Let's say someone gives us a piece of work they have just completed and we notice immediately that something looks horribly wrong with it. Our normal reaction might be to say "You've done it wrong!"

Maybe what we say is less blunt than this but this is the way it might be understood — a judgement of the person and/or his work. What is their reaction likely to be? If nothing else, it will be an unhappy feeling inside. It could even lead to more negative consequences, which is not good for them, nor for us.

So, how could we do this differently?

Supposing we say: "Thanks for this but something does not add up here. Now, you are the one who has worked on it, so perhaps there is something I have missed or misunderstood. Can you please take me through the figures (or process) and help me understand better?"

People are happy to help, so this will be far less likely to cause a negative reaction. Apart from that, there are two possible outcomes:

1. As they explain it through, they realise there is an error, and say so. "Oh?" We reply. What is it?" They explain it through and we can confirm with "I see what you mean. What you are saying does make sense." Most probably, they will themselves take it away to correct it.

The outcome is we did not tell them they were wrong. We did not judge them or their work. They discovered the error and they decided it must be put right. They have judged themselves and they want to correct the mistake themselves.

2. The second possibility is that, as they explain, we realise we had in fact misunderstood something and what they have done is quite correct. We can happily say: "ah! That is what I did not understand. Now it is clear. Thank you!"

... And we do not have "egg on our face" for misjudging someone's work!

In the process of trying to find a way of avoiding judgement of people, I can confirm that this approach has had positive results where people realised their own error and most certainly saved me from more than one "egg on my face" where I was in the wrong!

"Ask! Don't tell!" helps keep positivity in our communications with others. It demonstrates we are trying to understand. We really are listening to what they are saying — to the extent of seeking to understand what they mean as opposed to jumping to conclusions based on what we think they might mean.

It is a method that helps people to think things through more carefully and more fully and this is why it is of great help to use it for the discussions with our direct reports on their priorities and their action planning.

It is all aimed squarely at helping them be successful — Pioneering Powerful Performance.

Let us now take a look at how this can be achieved.

# 1.5. Action Planning using "Ask! Don't tell!"

Having asked our direct reports to identify some key areas for improvement and to create some plans for achieving that improvement, the next stage is to discuss these plans. In so doing, our role is that of facilitator. We need to guide them through a thinking process to enable them to evaluate their ideas and, at the same time, help them adopt this as part of their regular daily routine.

What follows in the next section is a suggested outline for this, together with some ideas for phrasing "Ask! Don't tell!" questions that will help the process. Obviously, we will need to adapt them to our own personal style but it is important to ensure we stay well within the "Ask! Don't tell!" philosophy.

Some of the questions listed in the KRA Meeting Guidance Notes refer to certain parts of the action plan format illustrated a little earlier.

**KRA Meeting Guidance Notes.**

*Introduction.*

**1. The Purpose of the meeting.**

For us all to plan how to align to, and focus on, company objectives so we are all pulling in the same direction using the KRAs.

- Support the quest for continuous improvement.

- Provide a platform and process for you to record achievements.

- Plan a way forward for your growth and development.

- To take us from "ordinary" to "extraordinary"!

**2. Some other points.**

- This process is new to us all and will take time to get used to.

- However, it is flexible enough to allow us to change it for the better as we go along.

**3. How we will proceed from here.**

- For the one or two priority items you have selected, I want to learn what it is and what makes it high priority. (Where we are now vs. where we should be.)

- Step-by-step, how you plan to address this.

- How you want to measure progress to ensure it is working the way you want it to.

- What support you will need from me to help you achieve your goal.

## Handy Questions (Supporting Ask! Don't tell!)

### 1. For this, we must adopt a Problem Solving approach.

To develop people's ability to tackle problems effectively we need to guide them through the following process and ensuring we neither pass judgement nor criticize them.

- Understanding the problem and its implications.
- Ensuring they have established the real cause(s) – WHY-WHY (See also Chapter 2.4.1 on Problem solving in a team environment.)
- Creating a number of alternative solutions.
- Evaluating the positives and negatives of each alternative.
- Assessing the potential damage of the identified negatives (likelihood/severity).
- Evaluating whether these negatives can be prevented/overcome/lessened (further problem solving).
- Deciding on the most appropriate way forward (Action Plan).

### 2. The initial stage.

- What are the one or two priority items you have identified and what KRA do they affect?

### 3. Looking at the priority item in more depth.

- What are the main reasons why you ranked this as the highest priority?
- What is the current situation?
- What is this costing in time, money, quality, delivery times, etc? (Quantify/qualify as accurately as possible.)

- How is this impacting any other KRAs? (Quantify/qualify as accurately as possible.)

- What do you envisage should be the objective/result/target for this? (To be entered in the Action Plan Objectives. Quantify/qualify as accurately as possible.)

- If you were to achieve the target, what would be the benefits? (To be entered in the Action Plan Benefits. Quantify/qualify as accurately as possible.)

- What are the various solutions you thought of?

- Please summarise the solution you plan to adopt.

- What reasons made you select the one you did rather than any of the others?

- Take me step by step through the action plan you have put together for tackling this.

- Roughly how long will each step be likely to take? (Enter start/end dates for each step in the plan.)

- Why?

- What do you anticipate might slow your progress or prevent you from succeeding?

- How do you plan to deal with these barriers? (Such plans will either be separate or, more likely, their actions incorporated into the action steps of this one.)

- What support do you need from any other department or person for any part of the plan? (Will need to be entered as an action step with that person's name in the "BY" column. We also need to get their initials/agreement and give them a copy of the plan.)

- Have you discussed it with them to seek their support? How have they responded?

- What do they need you to do to make it easier for them to help you? (Will be an action step to include at the appropriate point in the plan.)

- What can I do to help you be successful? Do you need any resources, action on my part, training, or experience? (Will need to be entered as an action step with our name in the "BY" column. We also need to initial/agree and have a copy of the plan.)

- You will need some milestones to ensure your work is producing the desired results.

- How do you propose to keep track of its progress — that it is going in the right direction and at the pace you want?

- What will tell you whether or not it is producing the results you seek?

- These checks should also be included in the Action Plan Steps.

**Closing.**

- Please let me have a copy of each of these plans so I know what you are trying to achieve.

- Please also ensure those involved have a copy and remind them to diarise their input so they can plan around it effectively.

- One last, but very important point: if you find things beginning to slip or you hit a roadblock you did not anticipate and you are unsure what to do, then let me know quickly so we can put our heads together to see what solution we can find.

Thank you ... And good luck!

# 1.6. Building a monitoring system.

*SYNOPSIS:*

*To ensure things are moving towards results, we need a positive and non-threatening monitoring system. To be effective, we must understand and set up three kinds of monitoring.*

-=.-=.-=-

There are three kinds of monitoring necessary to check we are on track:

|      |                                                    |
|------|----------------------------------------------------|
| i.   | Ensuring the action steps are rolling out as planned. |
| ii.  | Ensuring the expected results are happening.       |
| iii. | Ensuring the results are maintained.               |

## *i. Ensuring the action steps are rolling out as planned.*

This is the initial area of focus: are we doing what we planned to do? If not, then we cannot expect anything to change.

For the individual who "owns" the plan, the "Start Date" in his/her diary is the reminder to start the activity concerned. To increase effectiveness, the "End Date" will need to be in the diary twice, not once. It must first appear as part of the "Start Date" narrative so the full picture as regards timescale is clear at the outset. It might be an entry for 3rd May, "Compile a spread sheet list of customers showing their location, order sizes and frequencies over the past 12 months to be ready for analysis by 30th June." The second mention of the "End Date" will of course be written under 30th June.

For ourselves, we need to be able to keep a weather eye open to ensure the various plans being undertaken across our area are moving on schedule and nothing is overlooked. Naturally, this must be undertaken in a positive way so we do not make people feel they are being watched like a hawk!

The ideal situation is that a direct report will be comfortable being open about the situation, raising the alarm when things are not going as expected and ask for guidance or support as needed.

The criticality, and/or time criticality of a project, will determine the frequency of a formal or semi-formal report. A monthly formal summary may well suffice for most cases. See the suggested format on the following page.

Figure 2: Sample Action Plan Summary Format.

**ACTION PLAN SUMMARY**

Department: _____    Month/Year: _____

Name: _____    Position: _____

(Enter in Start Date order)

| Start Date | APlan No/ Step No. | Priority | Action Step | Target Date | Date Complete | % Done & Notes |
|---|---|---|---|---|---|---|
| | | | | | | |
| | | | | | | |
| | | | | | | |
| | | | | | | |
| | | | | | | |
| | | | | | | |

# 1.7. Stop here!

Stop reading any further for the moment, that is. The next step is in fact to go back to the first chapter of this book and start putting these initial ideas into action, getting the feel of it and turning it into more of a habit before moving to the deeper waters.

By all means consider getting a copy of this book for each member of your team so they understand what you want to achieve with them. By seeing and understanding the purpose and the philosophy behind what you want to bring into effect, they are likely to realise it is not change for the sake of change. It is not something being foisted upon them for ulterior motives. In fact, they should see it can help them have more influence and decision-making in their jobs as well as having their achievements recorded.

It should also be noted that they are likely to find their work more fulfilling, more fun and can even help in preventing stress.

This might well make the change easier because they will want the same results.

Once you and your team are more comfortable with adapting to a new way of working, you can all move forward to the next part - "Getting Deeper".

## *Yes, but …*

Yes, no doubt you will want to at least read the rest of the book first in order to understand the full process and approach to ensure you are comfortable with it all before taking the plunge. This short chapter is to draw a firm line to help prompt you into avoiding the temptation of trying to dive into deep water before practising in somewhat calmer seas.

## *Note:*

You may find the next, blank, page useful for jotting down notes and ideas on how you propose moving ahead with your team(s).

# Notes & References for Action.

# Part 2: Getting Deeper.

## 2.1. Getting more than just a vision.

*SYNOPSIS:*

*Creating a vision together with the team can provide a much more powerful way forward and gain a great deal more traction.*

-=.=.=-

We saw in Part 1.1. that creating a vision for our area — what we are really there to achieve — can focus our team and provide a united approach to achieving something. We saw how it can become a part of our "vocabulary" and on everyone's mind. On everyone's lips and, most importantly, in everyone's actions.

It was also shown that, as their manager, we will need to live it, breathe it, eat it, dream it. We must make it fun and exciting, not just a mantra that is repeated over and over without thinking. Celebrate the successes as they happen.

Let's dig in deeper now.

Wouldn't it be great if we did not have to "sell" the idea to our team? Supposing they could pick it up and run with it for themselves? What a difference that would make! Imagine the potential if they drove it instead of us having to do so?

There is a way of achieving this.

We can explain to them the elements of Forward Focus: the stakeholder demands and the balance required. We can show them how these break down into the six KRAs. We can ask them where they think we are currently weak so we can set priorities.

From there, we can ask them to go away with this information and think about a vision statement for our area — something that we will be proud to achieve together. At the same time, we should fix another meeting (not too far into the distance, or things might get forgotten) for airing the ideas and working together on a final agreed vision.

Some managers may fear losing control by apparently handing over to their subordinates such an important piece of managerial work. "Supposing they come up with something that is wrong?" "What if they miss out something important?"

As managers, we tend to forget that we were once in their position and no doubt had ideas about what we should be doing, what we could do better, and so on. Have you experienced this? Maybe your manager refused to listen? Maybe s/he tore your idea to pieces, making you feel you should never try voicing an idea ever again?

How would you have felt if your manager had listened? What would you have thought if the idea was evaluated with you and, if appropriate, taken to the next stage? I suspect you would be a bucket-load more positive than if you were not listened to or had your idea torn to shreds! What kind of effort would you put in to make sure the venture was successful?

So why don't we give our direct reports a chance to really contribute in order to take our collective performance to new heights?

Wishful thinking? Let me illustrate with another, very live, example in the next section of this chapter. It was written by a Senior Manager whom I was "virtual" coaching and who very kindly gave permission for me to reproduce it here.

**A live case study.**

*SYNOPSIS:*

*This live case demonstrates how powerful a team approach to a vision and focus can be. It is from a senior manager who used "Leading from Behind" and "Ask! Don't tell!" to create a vision and achieve high morale and engagement from a previously discouraged and unhappy team.*

-=-=-=-

## 1. The situation.

When I was hired into the company, my first assignment was to set up and to organise the new packaging department of the production site. Another one would follow, according to the company's plans. I was informed the company was putting a lot of hope for its growth on the new packaging departments.

After I had organised the packaging department and whilst waiting for the "green light" from the managing director of the company to start interviewing personnel for it, some decisions directly or indirectly taken by the top management unfortunately created a very bad atmosphere in the production site. People were not only disengaged and with low morale but, even worse, there was almost a workers' revolution in the production department. A very tough and unpleasant situation.

In the face of even bigger problems and consequences for the operation of the production department (the situation was no longer under control), the Managing Director asked me one day if I could take over the management of all people and try to improve the situation. "Please do your best" was the final comment.

Thus, I agreed to take over and do my best to put out the fire, so to say.

## 2. The approach.

Facing a situation in which everyone was going his/her own way, without any communication among people, with very bad interpersonal issues and more, the first thing I decided to do was to establish communication. One day I called everyone together and talked to them openly about the

45

situation, the consequences this might have for the company and, as a result, also for their jobs. I asked them that we try, all together, to create a better future for them … for us.

Two of the people approached me at the end and said that they were very pleased that someone had spoken to them.

"A good sign", I thought.

But it was at the same time obvious to me that those people were lacking communication. This assumption of mine was confirmed a few days later when I invited each worker to my office to have a one-to-one discussion with them. This was to get to know each individual better and hear what they had to say (their concerns, their problems, etc.).

After this first approach I kept thinking what to else to do in order to create harmony and a spirit of co-operation. The production had to keep on running, people problems had to be solved, improvements should be achieved.

Then I decided to build a team with the supervisors of the various departments. The idea was to create team spirit, good communication and other values in this team and then expand this also to the rest of the staff.

Furthermore, without having a core team with good morale and committed to a common goal, not much could be achieved in terms of productivity improvements and the like.

The team was built and we started having a formal meeting once a week. Initially, we were discussing problems the team members were presenting and they were all encouraged to suggest solutions. Soon I started talking to them about cost savings and their importance for the company (and of course for ourselves), especially due to the tough financial situation the country is currently in. I proposed, and they agreed, that we start working on cost savings projects. Another team member liked the idea and volunteered to take ownership of three of the projects which were proposed by us all.

But I felt there was something still missing in the team. Although morale seemed to have improved, I wanted to build a strong commitment towards a common goal. It was important that this should not take too much time and it should be achieved in order to create processes and obtain results that would be sustainable in the long term.

Whilst thinking what and how to do this, I asked Nigel for his assistance which he gladly offered. Very soon, Nigel asked me the following question:

"What is your vision for the area you are responsible for? Can you sum it up in a short sentence?"

I was caught by surprise by this because I hadn't thought of a vision as Nigel meant it (as it turned out during the "discussion").

The "dialogues" which follow have played a decisive role for my actions.

Me:

"My vision is:

To create a "team culture"

To increase the profitability of the company by cost reduction projects

To have the best people possible"

Nigel:

"What you have listed is what you want to have. It is more than a sentence and it does not make me feel that I want, I must, be a part of the action as an employee reporting to you. Please think about what we do for the customer, the team, the shareholders, our suppliers.

"Are you there just to make profits? Or are you there to provide something important to customers?

"The vision needs to be short as it serves as a kind of rallying call. A question we ask as we do things: 'how will this prove to our suppliers, customers, staff, and shareholders we are the package of choice?'

"How can we ensure our customers see us as the choice package? Is there something else we can do that will ..., How will this affect our staff's vision of us as ...

"It becomes a part of your "vocabulary". On everyone's mind. On everyone's lips. In everyone's actions.

"You will need to talk the talk, walk the talk, stalk the talk (openly recognise people as they do things that enmesh the vision = positive conditioning).

"You will need to live it, breathe it, eat it, dream it ....

"Make it fun and exciting, not just a mantra that is repeated over and over without thinking. Celebrate the successes as they happen".

Me:

"OK, I shall do some brainstorming. I find this statement very very challenging knowing the current situation in my company. What do you think of: 'Be recognised by our customers as their best supplier and by our suppliers as their best customer!'"

Nigel:

"Yes, it is good. Please, however, do not ask me to judge what is 'right' or 'best'. You are in the situation, it is for you to decide. You know far better than I ever could. My suggestion is that it should not be something that only challenges you. It needs to be something that can light up the eyes of everyone in the teams, and can permeate thinking and actions in the manner I described. It may not happen immediately, of course. You will need to walk the talk ... live, breathe ... etc ".

Me:

"What I feel I should do first is to establish trust among all people in the production site. They have been mismanaged in the past. I have the feeling they need someone to believe in. This is already achieved with four people (supervisors) and there is more progress than I expected in such a short period of time since we built that team. We already have an improved situation. What I am missing at the moment is engagement by all people. Motivation is also a big issue. What motivates each individual?

"I see the necessity to create a vision statement. A vision that will create positive mood. A vision which will help them to get rid of feelings of fear and have something to look forward to. A vision which will underline what we altogether as ONE should achieve if we want our company to survive in the very competitive environment.

"Then, after the vision statement is chosen, I will ask them all how THEY think we could turn the dream to reality (make what now seems impossible ... possible)."

Nigel:

"What motivates a person? Well, my suggestion is to forget motivational theory and 'Lead from Behind' as I term it. I can expand on that later if you wish".

Me:

"After I discussed the topic 'Vision Statement' with the supervisors etc and mentioned a bad and a good example of a Vision Statement, I asked them if they could help me phrase OUR vision statement. They asked for about a week to think about it and come with proposals/ideas. So next week we have a meeting on this issue".

Then Nigel sent me a couple of pages from his draft of this book and I particularly liked the following statement based on Peter Drucker's work:

*"So all we need to do as managers is to understand what is preventing them from performing the way they want to and help them remove the obstacles. Then they will automatically perform better." [Op. cit.]*

48

Peter Drucker was right. When there is a problem which seems to affect the performance of an employee we often try to fix the employee rather than the problem! And this is a mistake. I was very happy to read this because deep inside me this is what I am trying to find out myself. How to help people remove their obstacles. Let me give you a real life example of what happened recently.

When I asked our team members to help me phrase a vision statement for our production site everybody was listening carefully and were trying to understand what I meant by "vision statement". After mentioning two examples and they seemed to understand what I was asking for, one of them, a truck driver, said "But what you ask for is probably your vision because you have dreams for making a career."

"It is nothing to do with that," I replied. "However, I must admit that I fell into this trap myself over the weekend when I was trying to phrase a vision statement by myself. Therefore I stopped trying to phrase according to what would be wishful for me alone, because it should be our vision and not my vision. We will achieve more results with our teamwork if it does not matter who will get the credit at the end. If the team succeeds, every team member will succeed".

The truck driver then said "OK I understand and agree. But we will have to overcome obstacles so our vision will be impossible to achieve".

"Please do not think about obstacles. Let us create a vision statement first without thinking about obstacles. When and if serious obstacles arise we will face them together as a team."

"But I am a truck driver and I have learnt as a child to do things step by step," he pointed out.

"A step by step approach is very good. But we can talk about this again when we start discussing how to implement our vision".

The truck driver agreed.

A day or two later, I was sitting opposite the truck driver and we had a chat about his previous job. He told me that he was a ship commander and travelled a lot. He enjoyed charting the courses of the ship.

He was talking enthusiastically about his experiences and I thought of using this opportunity to inspire him to see an analogy between that job and the implementation of our vision. By doing this, I hoped to gain his better understanding of the reason for a vision statement and his commitment for the implementation. I therefore asked him if he used a compass for mapping the ship's course.

"Of course! Otherwise I would not be able to find our destination to Cephalonia." (A Greek island).

"So you knew where you wanted to go and had to chart the route and also use a compass so that you did not miss your destination?"

"Exactly!" He remarked. "And furthermore, if I had no support from the other ship staff and if not everyone was alert in a crisis situation, we would possibly have our ship sink. This is why I appreciated our team work. Because it reminds me of my time on the ship..."

I informed Nigel about this, in my opinion, very interesting discussion.

Nigel:

"One thing you have learnt is how much the truck driver values teamwork. It appears to be one of his core values. An important piece of information for you to ensure he is in a position to be a part of a team so he can have what he enjoys, knowing he will play his part too. And if you need to enlist his support in discussions about planning, you can speak of needing to chart a course towards an objective. You can refer to monitoring regularly to ensure we are 'on course' so we do not 'drift' and miss our planned destination."

How true. The truck driver has been the most devoted team member. I suggested that he made a presentation to the rest of us about how they used to work on the ship, which he gladly did and which was an inspiration for many new ideas.

Another concept which Nigel suggested and which proved to be extremely effective both in problem solving situations and also in brainstorming sessions with the team, was his "Ask! Don't tell!" concept.

According to this concept one avoids telling the team members what to do and especially how to do something. For example a team member comes with a problem. Instead of his manager telling him how to solve it, he asks questions, so that the person is facilitated to use his brain and come to a workable solution himself.

The "Ask! Don't tell!" concept worked well and was very effective in many situations. A very powerful methodology!

It proved to be effective not only during problem-solving sessions but also during other discussions. As a result of the above-mentioned approach we soon had a team with:

- a vision (proposed by the team),

- ground rules (e.g. "each team member is committed to help and support any other team member if and when needed", "our strength lies in mutual support and collaboration" etc.) and

- core values (e.g. team spirit, responsibility, integrity, consistency, cooperation etc.).

Both the vision statement and the core values were hung on a wall so that everyone could see them as a reminder.

Furthermore, I asked them to answer (on paper) two questions:

*Question 1: "What are those things you would "suffer" for"?*

*Question 2: "What are those things which would cause you to "suffer", if you did not achieve them?"*

By asking those two questions I wanted to get an idea of how far they were committed to our vision statement, how decided they really were in going for it and also how "ambitious" they were. From their answers I knew, more or less, what to expect from each one of them.

During our weekly meetings the team members were encouraged and facilitated to make suggestions for improvements. They were asked to set time-lines for each project for which implementation had been decided upon. After each meeting I was writing the minutes and was giving a copy to each of them.

Furthermore, we established KPIs (Key Performance Indicators) for each department, as well as an action plan. Results would be presented and discussed at the end of each month by each team member.

Within about 3 months of when it all started, we already had some remarkable results. The morale of the team was very much improved. Furthermore, they all became committed to a common goal. The first significant cost savings were achieved. The team members were always supporting and helping each other whenever needed. A very good communication was established between them.

Also, and very importantly, I kept on walking the talk and I was always available to support and guide them when needed by them. Without me giving the first example (i.e. doing what I was preaching), they would most probably not feel inspired and motivated to move to action.

During one of our team meetings the Production Supervisor asked how we could also motivate the workers towards our vision. This was a very good question and we all immediately agreed to support the Production Supervisor in engaging his workers.

First, I asked the Production Supervisor what the current situation was.

He explained that he had problems with his workers. Either they showed no interest in their work, or they would not listen to him (even not talk with him), or they were being very rude.

(In the meantime I had received a copy of the problem-solving workshop method from Nigel's draft book.)

Then, I asked the Production Supervisor who was (or were) the most difficult one(s) and why. He mentioned 2-3 names. I invited him to a one-to-one session and asked: "What do you think are the reasons for their behaviours?"

He gave a few possible reasons which I wrote down.

Then I gave him the piece of paper and asked him to think how he would like to approach each one of the people in order to resolve with them the reasons he considered the root cause for their behaviours.

"Please think about it and we can discuss again", I said.

He seemed to agree, yet he never decided to adopt this approach. Whenever I asked him for a meeting in order to discuss his issue further, he seemed (by his facial expressions) not to really want it. I could not figure out why. From a couple of informal one-to-one conversations which we had, I understood that there was hardly any communication between him as the Production Supervisor and most of his workers. As a result, they actually had no supervisor.

During the next core team meeting we all discussed again how to help the Production Supervisor achieve a turnaround with his workers. I suggested that we did an exercise together which would also benefit the other team members. The subject of the exercise was: why subordinates might not obey their supervisor.

A brainstorming session followed and all ideas were written on a flip chart.

This session intended to help the Production Supervisor understand or eventually realise why his workers were not following his instructions and did not listen to him and, even worse, why a couple of them would not talk with him or would even become rude and aggressive.

A further exercise we undertook was: 'What describes an organised workplace and what describes a workplace that is not organised?'

Again a brainstorming session followed and the team members were facilitated to express their opinions which were also written on a flip chart.

During both exercises I noticed the team members were asking him questions about certain things and, in so doing, used terminology such as "do you apply this? Why don't you do this?" "You must do this and that," etc. It was not only the questions they asked or the statements they made but, most importantly, the judgemental tone in their voice, facial expressions and body language. I could see that the Production Supervisor did not feel comfortable. He is the kind of person that can only be inspired.

I facilitated the discussion by reminding them that "we are all committed as a team to mutually support each other whenever needed. In this situation the Production Supervisor needs our help and support to overcome a serious obstacle he is facing. This time it is the Production Supervisor who is facing the problem, next time anyone of us could be in his position. We should therefore try to be more supportive than judgemental".

After we had finished both exercises, I suggested that we let a couple of days pass so that everyone had the time to think about the two exercises and allow everything that was discussed settle in their heads.

A few days later, during a one-to-one with the Production Supervisor, I asked him what he thought about our last session. He seemed to be very sceptical. I then asked him how he would prefer to continue his efforts for resolving his problems with his people. "Would you feel more comfortable if we continued as a team, or would you prefer to discuss only with me?"

He replied that he enjoys the team meetings but that he would prefer to discuss his current situation only with me.

On learning about this, Nigel suggested an exercise which I found very interesting. This exercise could possibly help and inspire the Production Supervisor to realise what leadership style he used to apply and what the expected results might be depending on the style he used.

I told the Production Supervisor about the exercise and, although he was convinced that he was leading in the right way, he accepted that we ask his workers to undertake this exercise in order to find out how they think. The exercise was as follows.

Assume we have three basic leadership styles:

- The supervisor decides everything without considering his subordinates' opinion.

- The supervisor asks for the opinion of his subordinates but he makes all decisions

- The supervisor asks for his subordinates' opinion and allows them to make decisions on their actions.

The Production Supervisor was asked to write down which are the most important qualities he would like his team to have. The following day, after thinking it through, he gave me a list he had compiled of the desired qualities:

- Hard working,

- co-operation,

- willing to work without having to be pressured to do so,

- responsibility,

- mutual respect.

"Now we will do the following exercise with your guys", I proposed to the Production Supervisor. I will write on a piece of paper the qualities you have given to me and ask your people when they think that these qualities would reach a high, moderate or low level, depending on the leadership style of their supervisor.

The Production Supervisor then explained that he had always used the style 2 (The supervisor asks for the opinion of his subordinates but he makes all decisions), which he thought was the best one. He definitely rejected style 1 (The supervisor decides everything without considering his subordinates' opinion).

He also stated he did not agree with style 3 (The supervisor asks for his subordinates' opinion and allows them to make decisions on their actions) because he thought that one should not let people take decisions on their own. He explained by saying "We do not have the time to talk for so long so that I can facilitate them to take decisions. Decisions on the field have to be taken within a few minutes."

I had a short but thorough discussion with him but I avoided telling him what to do and how to do it. Instead, I was asking questions which helped him to realise that many things are not as difficult as they may seem in the beginning. But first he must believe in it.

This is something magnificent, I learnt from Nigel's assistance: "Ask! Don't tell!" It is such a powerful communication tool.

The results of the exercise undertaken by the Production Supervisor's workers were very interesting (but not surprising).

- 5 out of 6 of the workers voted for style 3 (The supervisor asks for his subordinates' opinion and allows them to make decisions on their actions.)

- only one for style 2 (The supervisor asks for the opinion of his subordinates but he makes all decisions)

- Regarding style 1 (The supervisor decides everything without considering his subordinates' opinion), everyone commented that this style would be unacceptable and that a supervisor who applied it would feel very lonely …

I later discussed the results with the Production Supervisor, who was without doubt surprised. Yet, he kept on doubting that any of these reasons were the ones that caused him problems with his guys. Honestly, I must admit I started becoming impatient. However, I was thinking of other possible approaches.

During one or two informal talks with him and by using the "Ask! Don't tell!" concept, he seemed to understand that he should initially establish communication with his workers. I frequently asked him questions like: "How would YOU feel if …?", "How would YOU have reacted if …?", "Are these people different to you and I?", "Try and put yourself in their shoes," etc. etc.

During these talks I could see the Production Supervisor's face changing and becoming thoughtful. He seemed to realise …

Then there was a discussion about personal appraisal of the workers. I originally thought that it might be a good idea, so that I also have a better (and more objective) opinion about how each of the workers "thought". I then decided to ask the Production Supervisor to write down both the strengths and weaker points of each of his people. This was a last attempt to find out why the Production Supervisor was really complaining about regarding a few of them. He seemed to be very pleased with this proposal.

A few days later he came with his "appraisal". He had written down the qualities/skills his workers ought to have:

- Hard working,
- consistent,
- responsible,
- taking initiatives,
- honest,
- careful,
- obeying orders,
- team spirit.

Then, for each worker he placed an "X" below the quality he thought the worker had.

I said I thought he had done a good job of this and, knowing that it would help greatly to discuss why he thought that his workers had or hadn't the qualities he wished, I asked "Now, could you please tell me which of those qualities you consider to be the most important ones for the job those people are doing?"

"Hard working, responsible and careful", he replied.

After having a look at his scores, it was obvious that most of his people had those qualities. There were still a few who did not, according to his list. I suggested that he tries to establish a good communication with his people in the first place.

"But what shall I talk about with them?" He asked.

"What do you want to achieve?" I queried. "And what do you like about our team?" I continued.

He explained that he liked how much we support each other, especially in difficult situations.

"Do you think they do not need support?"

After thinking for a while, he said he would organise a meeting with his workers and discuss the planning of the forthcoming work activities with them. During this meeting he intended to ask them to plan those activities together, instead of telling them what to do.

Indeed, he did arrange the meeting a couple of weeks later. I was also present but only in order to see how the meeting went and to be ready to facilitate it in case of need.

The Production Supervisor did a very good job. Among other things, he told his people how much he values them and that he sees them as a team which has a common target. He said clearly that he will stand on their side and support them whenever they needed his help. Then he said that he would like to discuss the production plan with them and that he would like to hear their opinions about how to improve things by learning from mistakes of the past.

Interestingly, even those one or two people who were silent and sceptical during the earlier part of the meeting started sharing their views and talked about problems they faced the year before and made suggestions for improvements. When I noticed that my presence was no longer necessary, I said how glad I was that they are now all together as a team and I encouraged them to continue like this and also expressed my confidence that they would see positive changes in their work and in their relationship with each other. I then stood up and left the meeting.

Later on, the Production Supervisor came to my office with a big smile on his face.

"How did it go?" I asked.

"It went very well," he replied.

"From now on we decided to meet every 15 days," he continued.

"You did a very good job," I told him.

We then shook hands and he left in order to continue his vacation (which he had interrupted in order to have the meeting with his people).


*3. The results*


### 3.1. What was achieved?


My direct reports (the core team) had an improved morale level and were all committed to a common goal. Cost reduction projects were implemented and results achieved. Agreed targets for continuous improvement were established.

Furthermore, the Production Supervisor was facilitated to achieve a turnaround with his workers. He built a team with them and showed them that he values their opinion and their experience. He encouraged them to contribute to decision-making relating to their jobs. This approach had very positive results as one could observe in their reactions. The first change which the Production Supervisor soon observed in their behaviours was that they stopped continuously asking him (on purpose) what to do, in spite of the fact they very well knew how to do their job.

## 3.2. How was that achieved?

For achieving those results the strengths (and preferences) of each one of them were used but also mutual support and co-operation were encouraged in order to enhance the team spirit.

They were asked and encouraged to make decisions and if I thought that a decision was not the right one I tried to facilitate them to realise this by using the powerful concept: "Ask! Don't tell!"

What was also very important for them was that they knew I was always there to support and guide them when needed and if they made a mistake they knew that I would not blame them but I would discuss with them in a constructive way how to avoid making such mistakes in the future.

Conflicts (either within the team or between other people working in the production site) were always resolved in an effective way, so that trust was established, different interests and needs were taken into consideration — hence conflict escalations were prevented.

Ultimately, a pleasant workplace was created in which they all enjoy working.

Besides, I used every opportunity to mention (and explain) how important it was to achieve results (for the company as well as for us). My intention was to inspire them to become a results-oriented team.

---

*This live case demonstrates how the concept of not only building a vision but also the manner in which the senior manager treated his team began to cascade to provide a more positive environment for the next layer down. This generated a stronger team and a much more energised set of workers.*

*This is precisely what Pioneering Powerful Performance is all about.*

## 2.2. Stronger use of the KRAs.

*SYNOPSIS:*

*Once we and our team are more comfortable with the planning and monitoring process, we can start using them more powerfully, hitting problems and opportunities more strongly.*

-=-.=-.=-.

We can obtain far more of a grip on our work and especially our results by digging much more deeply into what the KRAs can help us achieve. What we looked at in Part I was just touching the surface, mainly to ensure we keep things simple and straightforward for getting us all used to the concept and to start focusing our thoughts and ideas.

It was aimed at someone either new to management, or new to the concept of Pioneering Powerful Performance, and starting the processes from scratch. It was suggested in Chapter 1.3. that we ask individuals to select one or two areas that they saw as priorities for improvement, commence drawing up plans and then following them through to reach the desired results.

Once this process is established, it is time to move from the shallows to the high seas. Why do I use this analogy? Two reasons. One is that the activity has been undertaken in a fairly shallow, although very positive and helpful, manner. This was preparing our vessel for the greater difficulties faced on the deep oceans.

The second reason is that it ties in with the prime responsibilities and activities of a ship's navigator who charts a course to the desired destination bearing in mind the potential risk factors, then monitors progress as the vessel progresses, and also adjusts the course depending upon events.

In the aforementioned chapter, we more-or-less started with the initial part of the navigator's role: charting out what to do about something of importance related to our results. We then went on to actioning it and also the monitoring of progress to check we were moving towards our planned destination and, if deviations arose through unexpected problems, re-planning actions to deal with them and get ourselves back on course.

Stage one was very superficially undertaken in order to keep things relatively simple and straightforward in order to inculcate the basis of the process. It was nowhere near being comprehensive and was carried out with only a touch of rigour or discipline. Yet this part of the entire exercise is one that, surprisingly, can really unearth an almost frightening amount of lost potential: collecting relevant information, ascertaining the risks and also the opportunities to determine priorities in readiness for the planning stage.

In the following chapters, we will take a much closer look at all of these aspects.

## 2.3. Ensuring the Sixes are Scored.

*SYNOPSIS:*

*Digging more deeply into each KRA to seek out problems and opportunities, remembering the importance of keeping them carefully balanced.*

-=.-=.-=-

For the first, the planning, stage we will need to take each KRA in turn and consider what kind of data we might need. We also need to think about how we can approach collecting and documenting them in a way that is simple yet provides valuable information. We do not want to fall into the trap of spending more time collecting data than we do in producing results!

These chapters will necessarily how we can start analysing the data to find opportunities and threats. This I find the exciting part because it so often presents us with a way forward for making substantial improvements in performance.

We must not forget the important aspect of ensuring there is balance between the KRAs and none is given extreme precedence at the cost of others. Because the cost savings element tends to be an example of this, we will look at a case or two that give stark examples of where undue stress on this KRA has caused strong negative repercussions on other KRAs — or even upon ongoing costs themselves.

Through all of this, we need to be mindful that our role as leader demands that we support our team to help them be successful.

## 2.3.1. Budget & cost control.

*SYNOPSIS:*

*Far too often, Budget & Cost Controls are excessively emphasised, throwing other KRAs (and therefore other stakeholders) into negative territory. To illustrate why caution is essential, some live cases are given to demonstrate how quickly and easily things can go terribly wrong as a result of such short-termism.*

*We then look at the kind of information we might need to collect, collate and analyse for this KRA.*

*One of the largest cost factors is generally that of staffing — a very contentious and emotional issue to deal with. We therefore look at some important preventive measures that are generally overlooked or, at worst, ignored.*

-=.=.=.-

This is the area that seems to get the most attention in companies. So often we hear of budgets being slashed, people being made redundant or, to put it in one of its many idioms, "letting people go".

Unfortunately, CEOs and/or other senior management decide, or have it decided for them, that profits must be increased, almost "at all costs". This can end up being done with little or no consideration for the other KRA items and is tantamount to short-termism — and short-termism too often leads to longer-term problems that end up being "all costs".

Focusing on the short-term is not only the province of senior managers. This debilitating disease can be found even at lower management levels. I have certainly witnessed it on a number of occasions.

Having been a "victim" of a "short-termist" manager, I can vouch for this. I was so disillusioned that I immediately sat and wrote a short story, a parody, from beginning to end to release my frustrations! *The Pyramid Factor* will be available later.[3]

In today's context, this kind of management can and does have a strong negative impact on staff retention.

> I was with the HR team in a fairly large organisation and they happened to start discussing and complaining amongst themselves about a fairly senior manager who was regarded by

[3] "The Pyramid Factor" — a parody of management *by Nigel J. Copsey.*

the board of directors as a great asset to the company because he regularly managed to obtain a high level of new business and was creating sizable profits.

The HR complaint was the amount of work he caused them. His area leaked people like water through a sieve and the recruitment team was forever trying to find, interview and recruit replacements — only to find they too would exit the company after but a few months. I questioned why this might be so and the answer was categorical. It was the way this manager treated them. He drove them far too hard and was forever berating them if they did not produce things as quickly and as well as he demanded.

Enquiring about their cost per hire and the number of replacements they had to recruit for him in a year, I suggested they "do the math" to get a rough idea of how much he was costing the company annually in staff attrition. The figure they arrived at was quite staggering.

"And he manages to get such high profits even after these expenses are charged back to his unit?" I asked in surprise.

The response was a blank, questioning stare from the team.

"Do you not charge back the costs you incur on his behalf?" I enquired.

They had no such system. HR was treated as a cost centre as opposed to being a service provider to the various parts of the business.

Because of this, the true state of that manager's unit Profit & Loss account was totally invisible. He was therefore being recognised and rewarded for something he did not in fact achieve.

This is a perfect (and true) example of how a focus on the KRA of revenues without properly assessing that of budget creates a completely misleading result.

Let's take a look at a case where the focus on cost-cutting (apparently to boost profit figures, although this is an employee's view rather than a proven fact) went to the silly extreme. It illustrates how over-emphasising one KRA can have negative effects on others, and may even be self-destructive.

The front tyres on my car were running a little low on tread and as we were hit by sudden, heavy, snowfall. I decided it was time to get those tyres replaced.

I called in at a local tyre service station, where they were slightly understaffed. They warned me that the wait would be about 40 minutes, so I went to sort out some other business first. On my return, I found they had closed the doors to the fitting bays but still had an "open" sign up. I thought perhaps they were keeping the place as warm as possible.

On enquiring in the office, I was told that they were not closed but they could not do any work. The reason was that the slope up to the fitting bays was so steep that cars could not get up it without skidding. Two customers had been perilously close to accident already.

"And they won't allow me to buy any grit," commented the manager with obvious disgust.

"How do they expect you to work, then?" I naturally asked.

He shrugged his shoulders. "That's their problem," he replied.

"And they only made £320 million profit last year," chipped in a fitter sarcastically.

"Yes, and I have a machine that has broken down. For three months it has been sitting there" added the manager scowling. "Because I am not allowed to spend out on getting it repaired, we are having to turn away business."

So, for the sake of a few pounds for a bag of grit, the business of that unit was at a total standstill. They wanted to work. They wanted to look after the customers. Instead, they sat there waiting to see if the snow would clear and, in the meantime, the company was paying them to get bored to tears.

As you can see, the miserly approach to budgets has led to revenues being lost, customer dissatisfaction (many would have to go elsewhere and they may well stay with their new supplier), staff morale dropping because they were keen but prevented from doing a good job, plus their growing lack of confidence in senior management and their decision-making capabilities.

The problem is that this kind of thing is too easily done and, from experience, I find it is generally the unyielding and "deaf-eared" cry for costs to be cut that management end up (literally) trying to "cut expenditure at all costs". In the process, they can end up spending far more than they had expected to save. This can take the form of being successful in cutting the costs of a particular budget heading but at the cost of a similar amount, or perhaps more, under another heading.

I recall such an "overdose" of cost-cutting when I was working overseas. Our central office apparently undertook a review of the servicing costs of air conditioning plants and units in the area. They decided that the manufacturer-approved company that supplied the air conditioning was charging far too much so tenders were invited. The cheapest tender apparently got the servicing contract.

Unfortunately, these "cheaper" engineers gave the distinct impression they did not really know what they were doing. The result? By saving on maintenance charges, we were hit with higher spare parts costs — and more breakdowns. The latter led to us having unhappy staff trying to work in the heat of a very hot summer, and the added costs of purchasing pedestal fans to try to make the offices a little more towards the tolerable.

I guess the air conditioning maintenance cost heading was down to the new target but the cost of repairs and spare parts was much higher and on top of this was the purchase costs of the fans. It did not do much good to the morale level of staff (myself included) forced to work in a stuffy office where the outside temperature was hitting well over 40 degrees centigrade in the shade.

This all goes to show that although cutting costs is important, it is vital that it is done in a careful and sensible manner and the potential impact considered prior to taking action.

## What should we consider measuring under this heading?

The most obvious and the easiest measure is the Profit & Loss account for our area, supplied internally through Management Information Systems. This will have all the costs under their various headings (e.g. rent, staff costs, stationery, etc.).

Unfortunately, not all companies provide any such information or they may have only limited feedback on departmental budgets giving some expenditure headings, such as stationery, but neither include a share of rent, utilities nor staff costs.

One department where this is often badly misapplied is HR, where there will be budget heads like training and development, which is a typical example of lack of either understanding of the business or of foresight. As

I touched upon a few paragraphs back, accountability is where it shouldn't be instead of where it must be.

HR department must have a budget because they too must be cautious about spending. Being a service provider, not a cost centre means that, in reality, the various units or departments actually incur the costs, not HR. This naturally means HR should calculate the costs of their various services and charge their "customers" for using them.

Such charge-backs to unit/department budgets will make a significant contribution to ensuring those who add real value are identified and considered for greater responsibilities. These are the leaders who will take the company forward. Those who are ineffectual will realise the true nature of management and resolve to improve — or leave to make way for someone who does.

However, unless we can influence those at the top, we have to live with these strange and debilitating anomalies but despite them we can still work on the basis of savings. Even though some may not apparently be reflected directly in our results, this does not prevent us from logging and reporting these achievements for ourselves and our team(s).

## *What data can we obtain?*

If the organisation furnishes us with a monthly Profit & Loss statement, we have a very good start. More likely, however, we will at best receive our expense statement, showing how much we have spent so far this financial year against budgeted figures for each expense heading.

What should we be looking for?

- The items to focus upon are the larger ones. Saving 10% of £10,000 is of higher value than saving 10% of £10 so, as the saying goes, we should pick the low hanging fruit first.

- It will be helpful if we can also review the costs this year against past years. What are the trends? Is the cost rising faster than it should bearing in mind inflation and by comparison with the volume of work being undertaken in the previous year(s)?

- Can what we do and the way we do it be changed to lessen the costs?

What is unearthed can at times be quite surprising.

> I had taken over a small office and was soon presented with the stationery order to sign off for the coming year. Glancing through it, I found it to be a little on the high side. The Senior Officer had presented it to me and he had worked there for many years. I was about to sign it on the assumption that he would know far better than I but I thought I'd just make one or two checks, just to be sure.
>
> I was taken to the stationery room in the basement and the relevant cupboards were opened for my inspection. Yes, they were low in stock. As the Senior Officer was locking the doors, I looked around the room and saw a number of large crates stacked in a corner. I asked what they contained.
>
> "Stationery deliveries," was the response.
>
> Puzzled, I arranged for a couple of crates to be opened. What I saw led me to ask for the others to be opened up.
>
> There were enough stocks of some stationery items to last us for several years! In spite of this, more were being requested in the order I had been asked to sign off.
>
> It seems the branch had been taking the easy way out by just repeating the same order each year without bothering to review of the stock in hand!

## The largest cost factor.

This is most likely to be staff costs. The very thought of examining and questioning this might cause us to feel ill at ease. The reason is straightforward: no-one likes to make people redundant.

However, we can look at this in a totally different light, which is a much more positive and constructive approach.

By creating spare capacity we can, for example:

- handle more work with the same numbers, perhaps even by taking over a process from some other hard-pressed area of the company if it makes sense to do so;

- get project work undertaken without disturbing the normal daily routine;

- allow time for development and self-development, including for those who aspire to a different role of some kind;

- avoid recruiting for expansion of an area in the company or for replacing retirees/leavers.

The process of re-placing staff and not recruiting to expand or replace those leaving because of retirement or (non-forced) exits is a relatively slow pace. However, it is also much more likely to fit with our gradual improvement in productivity. Being a trickle as opposed to a sudden mass reduction in numbers, it is more easily handled as well as being far less damaging to individuals.

By undertaking this kind of approach, we can ensure our part of the organisation is lean and competitive.

From what I have witnessed, the sudden directive to dramatically cut staff numbers can so easily lead to ineffective, inefficient and demoralising results. It will increase the potential for a longer-term problem. The remaining, demoralised, staff are not only likely to just do what is needed to keep their jobs, they will also be preparing to leave. They will be on their starting blocks, waiting for the market to open up again. Once this starts to happen, they will race off to a better place to work.

What is the impact? The market is gaining momentum and, as we are about to recruit extra numbers to help us cope, the older hands are rushing out of our doors. We are now faced with having to recruit replacements who will need training and settling in before they are productive.

The "top-down" direct orders can be very negative in impact and not just when cost-cutting.

I once overheard a senior manager telling one of his managers: "It's your problem, not mine. You tell me they won't do it but all you have to do is motivate them. You're their manager so go and motivate them!" Needless to say, he was not considered a great person to work for!

Unfortunately, this is the way some senior managers tend to operate. They seem to think that they have done their part by giving an overall instruction without considering the experience, knowledge or ability of the recipient. My own view on this, although somewhat sceptical, is that the senior manager hasn't a clue what to do about an awkward situation and delegating it removes the onus from his/her shoulders. It naturally follows that, if anything goes wrong, the blame can be placed squarely on the shoulders of the direct report.

I believe this type of management was typical during the recession in the 1990s in the UK when managers were told they had to reduce their staff numbers by a certain figure or percentage. As far as senior management was concerned, it was a case of: instruction given, my job done! I would venture to suggest that a fairly large percentage of line managers had neither the experience nor the expertise to approach this in a rational manner. As a result, what appeared to happen was that the staff numbers were reduced and the work reallocated amongst the remaining people. This naturally caused horrendous overloading and a great deal of stress. People did not dare refuse for fear of being sacked and ended up working long hours without a break and perhaps even at weekends too.

How many of us are taught any techniques or processes to enhance productivity? When we take over a management role from somebody else we tend to learn what they were doing and continue the same habits. If something goes wrong, we bolt on another step in the process to make sure it doesn't happen again.

If volumes increase we immediately call for additional resources in order to cope. Unfortunately, this can so easily have the undesired effect of over-staffing. Why do I say "unfortunately"? Apart from the unnecessary costs making the organisation less economic to run, during the recession it also leads to a larger number of people being made redundant.

Added to this, managers tend to grow the numbers rather than control them. Some even practise "empire building" — increasing the head count reporting to them purely in order to enhance their "responsibilities" and thus enabling a claim to have legitimacy in acquiring a higher ranking and/or pay level.

The result of these activities, wittingly or unwittingly undertaken, can cause so much damage during the tougher economic climates. I recall this vividly in the recession of the early 1990s in the UK. It led to a great deal of trouble for the people side of the business. Yes, there was the hammer blow for those being made redundant. Yes, there was a feeling of fear in those who remained. On top of this, a feeling of guilt was apparently found to exist with many who retained their jobs.

I had been through similar downsizing situations whilst working in India. Although redundancies were illegal, the cuts in head-count were made by not replacing those who retired and there was a steady flow of retirees. So we would suddenly be told we had to cut staff numbers "across the board" by 10%. This was an order and was non-negotiable. It caused a great deal of consternation: "how can I get the work of ten people done by only nine?" The only apparent way forward was to redistribute the work across fewer people, causing rumbles of dissatisfaction among managers and staff alike.

Fortunately, whenever I went into a new arena I was regarded as a bit of a nuisance because I questioned everything, much to people's discomfort. However, this questioning approach enabled me to uncover what had hitherto been unidentified opportunities. Streamlining processes not only makes them less expensive to run but can provide a quicker service to the customer. It also cuts the cost of producing the item, allowing us to be more competitive in our pricing without reducing our margins and still creating the same amount of profit, if not more.

This is the kind of thing we now need to inculcate into our direct reports. Instead of just one person (ourselves) looking for possibilities, we will end up with everyone trying to find things that will help improve everything we do. This is not just an idealistic way of thinking. Let me give you a very real example.

> When managing a branch office, I transferred a clerk from a job he had been doing for many years in order to give him a change. After ensuring he was carefully inducted and trained into the role, I mentioned to him that I didn't want him to "just do a job". If he had any ideas to improve things in any way, I would like to know about it.
>
> About three weeks later, he approached me with an idea for improving the stationery used for tallying the day's entries so that the process would take around 5-10 minutes instead of the current half-hour or so.
>
> The idea was sent to the Regional Manager's Office, which controlled the printing in the region and the idea was accepted. This resulted in the saving of 20 minutes per day per branch. Spread that across the 50 branches across the entire country and the savings really do become significant.

That is something that I would never have got around to noticing on my own!

We must therefore find a way of invoking change and improvement that takes into account people's experience and knowledge rather than just issuing the curt instruction "you had better improve it!" It will most certainly require extra input from ourselves but we must not lose sight of the fact that we are a part of the team in respect of getting results.

This should help us find ways to achieve optimal numbers.

Let us now take a look at some of the most critical questions we need to bring into play to make this happen.

## a. Who is doing what?

Do we really know who is doing what? Yes, we are aware that Jenny is team leader of invoice processing but what exactly is she spending her time on? Is she undertaking tasks that should be in the hands of a direct report rather than with her?

There are some managers or supervisors who find it difficult to "let go" of what they used to do before they were promoted. Often this is because they were so expert at the job that they find it difficult to delegate because of the worry it may not be done as effectively.

Although this is an understandable response to the situation, the question arises, in very blunt terms: why are we paying Jenny to carry out supervisory duties when she is spending a large part of her time doing clerical work? Is this also preventing her from doing what she should be doing and, if so, what are the consequences?

Many who fall into this trap may end up staying late and/or taking work home in order to ensure they do a proper job of it. This is neither healthy nor fair. I have seen it lead to quite serious problems on the home front, which is not the kind of outcome that is acceptable.

Others finding themselves under pressure might end up taking another route — they delegate upwards. Their manager has to chip in to help them take the strain. And here is also where the call for additional staff is also likely to be seen as the only solution.

Similar to this is the potential that those who are not leaders by nature are generally risk-averse and "protect" themselves by adding another layer of people beneath them to undertake additional checks to ensure no mistakes are made, thus bringing "safety" into the decisions they perforce have to make.

It is uneconomical to have managers spending their expensive time doing a chunk of the work of supervisors and for supervisors to be working on clerical processes. As mentioned, it can in some cases lead to dissatisfaction and family problems. It is not helping the individuals to grow nor can it be giving any sense of job satisfaction, let alone pride.

We must therefore invest time in finding out who is doing what. This reminds me of a situation that I faced with a couple of managers.

In one of my managerial roles, I was responsible for several functional areas and, in one area in particular, the two managers used to work late every night without exception. They would leave at 7.30 or 8.00 each evening.

I found this unacceptable and decided it should be tackled. However, I was also fully aware of the historical thinking that seemed to prevail: if you work late, you are showing your commitment to the organisation and you will be smiled upon. To tell the truth, it was more a case of: if you left at 5.30, you were asked whether you had enough work to do whereas if you worked late, you were "just doing your job" - it was nothing more favourable than that.

I arranged for us to sit together one evening to discuss the issue. "I am not happy that you leave the office so late. I want this to change so that you leave at 5.30 pm, latest at 6.00."

"But we have so much work to do," they objected.

"That is what we are going to discuss now to try to find ways to remove the pressure. My first objective is to get you out by 6.30 pm latest."

First, I requested them to outline the work they did. It transpired they were certainly doing a lot of work but a large proportion of it comprised tasks they should not have been doing. It was clerical rather than managerial and needed to be reallocated to their teams.

We then reviewed some major areas of the work of the department: their roles, the roles of everyone else in the department, the work that was being done and the way in which it was done. It resulted in discontinuing some processes where there was duplication or where it did not even need to be undertaken. It involved changing some processes to streamline them. This freed sufficient time down the line to enable delegation of the work the managers should not have been doing.

It took about a week or two to make the majority of changes. The Monday of the following week, both managers went home "early" at 6.00.

On the Tuesday morning, I made a point of going over to them and asking them how their Monday evening went. The response came with smiles that would have led one to believe they had been given an unexpected bonus!

"Last night I did something that I have wanted to do for years but have never had the time," said the more senior of the two.

"What was that, if you don't mind me asking."

"I went for a walk with my wife," was his reply.

I was delighted but also taken aback that such simple pleasures had been denied him for so long.

Although this streamlining sped up certain delivery schedules for our customers and, in effect made the department less expensive to run, if we think about this carefully, we will also notice that yet another KRA has been affected: "Staff Morale".

The three of us achieved it through a team effort whereas, if I had not used my experience and knowledge to assist the process, they would never have been able to obtain these results on their own. No end of bullying by me would have made any difference either!

## b. Why are they doing it?

This may seem to be a silly question but what is more surprising is the answer we get. It is not uncommon to find people are doing things because that is what they were told to do as part of the job when they took it over from their predecessor yet, on investigation, we find there is actually no reason for it to be done at all.

I have often found this to be the result of an error happening in the past. Something goes wrong, so an additional process is added to prevent it from occurring again. Quite a number of bolt-on activities can end up creating a good deal of work but, when we delve into analysis, we may well find the reasons now defunct or the additional activities were total overkill.

A simple example …

I took charge of a small administration unit and noticed a senior clerk received a large internal delivery envelope from which he removed a computer report that was a good 3/4 inch in thickness. He took it to one of the filing cabinets and filed it away, removing a previous one that he dropped into the "for shredding" bin.

Out of curiosity, I asked what the item was and what it is used for.

He told me it was a copy of a monthly report sent to one of the departments. He did not know what that department used it for. So I asked him why we had a copy. It seems that, once upon a time, that department did not get their copy and some important task could not be undertaken as a result. To prevent this from happening again, it was decided to have a separate copy sent to ourselves as a backup.

So, every month, this thick wad of paper was being created, enveloped, and sent for us to file for a month, after which it would be put through the shredder to be replaced by an updated copy.

This did not make sense to me. I decided to call our IT people. I gave them the monthly report reference number and mentioned they were sending a copy to us and I wanted to understand why this was happening. Their answer was that they were instructed to do so. I questioned whether, if the report for a specific month was misplaced and required some months later, could it be easily reproduced. The answer was affirmative.

The monthly delivery to our unit was stopped and saved some time in IT department as well as in ours, and also stopped the wastage of so much paper every month.

A much more significant situation was brought up as a "problem person" challenge in a Problem Solving Workshop I ran as part of a Management Development Programme.

A manager stated he was having trouble with a member of staff who complained bitterly about being given a certain role, which he found boring, repetitive and "a waste of time". The manager had explained to him that it had to be done and most of the others had had to do it. Now it was his turn.

The manager advised us that the clerk had become difficult to deal with and, on top of that, was often absent from work. He was taking sick leave and casual leave and, as a result, there was a backlog steadily building up.

The Workshop process brought out some important points.

- The clerk viewed this job as useless and he felt he was merely acting as "a post office".

- No-one liked doing this job. It had always been difficult to get people to do it.

- The manager explained to us how the job was done, which was mainly a filing process.

- On being asked why the clerk saw it as a waste of time, the manager told us he had said "the information is already filed and updated in another location in our records, so why file it again elsewhere?"

This last point was analysed and it became very obvious indeed that the job was totally unnecessary. The clerk was right. The role gave no sense of satisfaction or self-worth, in fact, it brought negative feelings.

The task was subsequently stopped and not only saved the cost of a member of staff (who could now be used to do something much more productive and fulfilling) but also stopped the feeling of degradation of an incumbent.

Why something is being done should be considered whilst investigating who is doing what. There will be little point in getting someone different to do something that need not be done in the first place. There is no satisfaction in being made to undertake a "non-job".

## c. How are they doing it?

People inherit systems and processes and do not necessarily think about what they are doing. This is, of course, not necessarily their fault. Sometimes we are forcibly told by a boss to do what we have been told to do or, as one boss stated: "Your role is to get the job done. Leave the thinking to me!"

Another factor is in learning a new role; we focus on what we are taught to do. Then the work gets a bit more pressurised and we end up just battling to get the work through rather than having the time to think about the way we are doing it.

Questioning the "how" can bring these kinds of situation to light. Let me give an example.

One of my staff seemed to be taking a whole day to do half a day's work. He would quietly disappear from his desk for periods of time, I wondered if it was perhaps to have a quiet smoke. He would make a deliberate point of taking papers back and forth and I guessed he did this in order to throw me off the scent. In fact, he was even careful to ensure that he left a little late sometimes, presumably to make me believe that he was hard-pressed and should not be given any additional work.

I kept a note of what he actually achieved each day and this was evidence enough. I now knew the facts. It was time to have a chat about all this and get the issue sorted.

"Derek, I wonder if you can take me through something that mystifies me." I started carefully.

"Sure.  What is it?"

Well, I realise that I do not know how you go about processing that work you do. Can you run through it for me please?"

"No problem. Do you want me to do it step-by-step?" He asked.

"That would be great, thanks."

"It starts when I receive the relevant letters in the morning post," he explained. "I take them to the filing cabinets to dig out the files concerned" he continued, gesturing towards the door I had seen him disappear out of during the day.

"You pointed in that direction. Is that where the cabinets are?"

He confirmed this, so I asked if he could show them to me. He very willingly led me across the room, down two flights of stairs, through a long corridor to a block of four filing cabinets with four drawers each. He opened one of the drawers, which was literally crammed so tight with thick files that he struggled to pull one out to show me.

"Just a moment" I said. "How many of these drawers contain your files?"

"All of them," he replied.

I pulled open random drawers in all four cabinets to find each one was in the same state - jammed tight with files. "At a guess, how many of these cases are ones you do have to refer to?" I asked him.

Derek thought for a few seconds and said there were about 30-40 cases and that all the remaining files were completed ones.

In effect, he had to come all the way down here, wrestle with the filing cabinet contents, go all the way back up, work on the cases, then bring the files all the way down again and try to force them back into their positions against the will of the tight wad of files.

On top of all this, he had similar letters that came in from reception and/or the afternoon mail, telephone calls that required him to pull out and return files. No wonder he looked so fit!

We then sat and discussed this very point and between us came to the conclusion that it would make life far easier for him if the completed cases were bundled off to the archives and if the 30-40 files that were needed could be placed in a cabinet close to him.

Derek volunteered to get this work done and, after a few days, the stuff he needed was just an arm's length away from his desk.

The day after it was completed and working, Derek suddenly appeared in front of my desk in the early afternoon. "Excuse me interrupting, Nigel, but do you have anything else you want me to do?" he asked. "The thing is, you see, I have completed my day's work and have nothing else to do."

Thank goodness I used the "Ask! Don't tell!" approach rather than acting on my hunches or I would have unnecessarily created a great deal of ill will!

## d. When are they doing it?

The work to be processed in a day can be horrendously high at times. There are often peaks and troughs but it is the peaks that naturally cause the difficulties.

The average manager will cry out for a higher head-count so that these peaks can be dealt with. However, the result can easily be "over-staffing" during the troughs but, because this "cannot be avoided", it is accepted.

People may well stretch out the work during the quieter times because they have nothing else to do but what effect is this having on our costs?

We might be able to consider building an agreement with another department or area that has a different volume pattern so we augment each other's staffing appropriately but this is not always so easy. More often than not, the peaks will unfortunately coincide.

So now we should ask ourselves the question: "when are people doing the work?" The next question is "Why then?" Let me illustrate with another live example.

In the bad old days before computerisation in the banks in India, customers' standing instructions for payments to be made from their accounts to beneficiaries (e.g. subscriptions, rent, etc.) was all undertaken manually. This involved a clerk having to pull out the relevant information cards for today's date, create the voucher to debit the customer's account and prepare a bank cheque and covering credit slip for the beneficiary's account at another bank.

The trouble was that the majority of payments were to be made at either the start of a month or the end of it. The peak was therefore spread over about a week or two — several days either side of the month-end. The clerk concerned had difficulties with this and, as other staff were facing peaks at this time, no assistance could be provided. The overload led to delays and, because of this, a few customer complaints.

Thus, timeliness of service was negatively affected, as was staff morale.

Something had to be done. Applying the "Who is doing it?" and "How is it being done?" produced nothing helpful. We then thought about "When is it being done?" and looked at his volume levels for a few months. This analysis showed that the middle of the month was relatively low volumes and the clerk agreed he was by no means stretched during that time. We therefore decided he would start preparing payments in advance, which would be securely kept until the due date, then issued.

This action led to his work being evenly spread across the entire month and comfortably so. He was relieved not to have to face the pressure of the month end and customers' payments were sent out well in time, preventing complaints.

# Conclusion.

These are some of the ways in which staff costs can be reduced or controlled, preferably by not recruiting for leavers or by ensuring we do not unnecessarily recruit more than are really needed.

These methodologies of reviewing both the work and the workloads should always be in the back of our minds because we are unlikely to capture all possibilities in one review. Being alert to the possibilities will help us find more potential as time goes on. Some of the useful data to collect are:

- Monthly costs by category
- Volume of items processed, by their nature, by day, week, month
- Who is doing what?
- Why are they doing it?
- How are they doing it?
- When are they doing it?

Improving productivity brings benefits to all the stakeholders of the business. Unfortunately, the word "productivity" has negative connotations because it has been linked with "rationalisation", "reorganisation" or, to give the real underlying flavour, "redundancies".

As we have seen from the above examples, this needn't be so. Also bear in mind that staff numbers can be reduced in a very humane fashion such as not recruiting replacements when people leave the organisation, especially if the productivity is improved over a fairly long period rather than being done in one fell swoop. And this is a big part of what we are trying to achieve here. We are preventing or lessening the potential for large-scale redundancy.

I would also like to add to the argument by suggesting that a lean, effective, efficient and economical business in which people are geared up to seek further improvements and embrace change, is likely to be one that stands better chances of survival during tough times.

There is only one major drawback in running a lean unit and that is in times of economic difficulty, a CEO may issue the strict and blanket edict to cut staff. Other parts of the organisation that have been carrying excess staff can do this more easily, whereas we are already at optimum and cutting will result in negative consequences for the business.

So, if you are a CEO or senior manager (or you become one) it will be important to know which parts of the organisation are run on a lean basis and, as importantly, those that are not. This will ensure cutbacks take place in the right places instead of in the wrong ones. Of course, identifying the less productive units will pinpoint where additional investigation might be needed to unleash the hidden potential.

## 2.3.2. Quality of our products/services.

*SYNOPSIS:*

*Quality control is not the sole province of manufacturing. It applies as strongly to other parts of the organisation and for similar reasons: low quality causes extra work, adds to costs, upsets and loses our customers.*

*We look at the data we need to consider under this heading, how to collect and analyse them to draw conclusions and find opportunities.*

*We illustrate some easy mistakes that can be made in this process and discuss how to avoid them.*

-=-=-=-

In manufacturing, there is normally a Quality Control unit that ensures the goods being made are to the exact specifications required by the customer. This is a process that is generally not restricted to checking the end product because, if it is found wanting, the potential cost of a total re-working of the items is extremely high. Normally, there are control checks at different stages or processes to ensure any deviations are caught very early and corrected. This is a far more economical route.

We also have to consider the fact that a total re-work may mean a late delivery which will carry the attendant risks of a cancellation or of losing the goodwill of a customer — or both.

However, in non-manufacturing areas or companies, in office situations for example, this kind of quality control is often lacking in spite of being most certainly of critical importance for the same reasons.

## *What we are looking at.*

First of all, we need to remember that our customer is not always external to the organisation. We may provide a service to other parts of the company. An example can be the Accounts or Finance Department, which provides other departments with monthly Profit and Loss or expenditure figures against budget. Another might be Training Department undertaking work for various units.

If an internal service is incorrect, it has implications upon the recipient unit and could lead them into making wrong decisions or actions. These in turn can adversely affect deliveries to external customers and/or endanger our profits and reputation.

Indeed, as with manufacturing, any mistakes we make have to be corrected and this re-working carries a cost factor.

This means we need to ensure the work we produce in our area must be free from errors.

A tall order?

No. A challenging goal! True, perfection is probably unattainable but zero defects is a target worth aiming for — within reason. The cost of controlling it as against the cost of it happening has to be borne in mind.

*There are three main areas that we need to focus upon.*

## i. Complaints.

First of all, we should record all customer complaints. What the complaint is then, after investigation and correction, what the cause was.

The analysis and process will be similar to that under our next heading.

## ii. Errors.

Similarly, we should also record any errors we find, again ensuring we enter the details of the cause.

Review and analysis of the causes is the next important step. This is followed by problem-solving, action planning, and the monitoring of results. In the problem-solving and action planning activities, it is vital that we remember that corrective action is only one part of the exercise. The part that is perhaps more important is prevention — ensuring it does not happen again.

To avoid "overkill" we need to evaluate carefully: was this a "one-off" cause and unlikely to happen again or is it potentially a recurring error and therefore demands action? Some items can be prevented by a slight tweaking of the system. The most awkward is where the underlying cause is human error. How do we deal with this?

Unfortunately, some managers react by criticising the person concerned and telling them they must improve. They will be satisfied perhaps by the response of "I will be more careful in future" or "I will try harder", both of which are generally quite useless statements. This is not because the individual won't bother but because they may not know how to prevent such things recurring.

For this, we must go back to an earlier statement made: "How many people want to fail?" This applies strongly in the case of errors. People do not want to make mistakes. So the way in which we as their manager deal with this is of paramount importance in order to ensure we do not diminish Pioneering Powerful Performance.

It may take a simple training exercise, explaining the "why" as well as the "how", followed by careful monitoring at the outset to ensure the lesson has been effectively learnt and applied.

A supervisor complained bitterly to me about the performance of one particular clerk. This clerk was the channel through whom the various kinds of items were passed on to the processing staff. His role was to check the items were all present and correct and were in a state that was in order for the processing work to be undertaken.

Unfortunately, the clerk was making innumerable errors, causing problems for the processing staff when they had started entering the item's details, only to find the remainder could not go through. The work had to be undone and returned for correction.

The supervisor had tried sitting with the clerk and explaining over and over how to deal with the different kinds of items but this had been to no avail. He wanted the clerk to be taken out of his department.

Because the clerk concerned was not a work-shy person but seemed unable to learn so much complexity quickly enough, I suggested a different approach be tried first — that the supervisor sits with the clerk again and take him, step by step, through the process required for each of the many kinds of transaction. However, this time he should get the clerk to make a checklist as they went along. This way, the clerk had a checklist for each kind of item he would encounter and noted in his own words.

The supervisor followed this suggestion and the clerk rarely made a mistake after that and it wasn't too long before he was getting the work through correctly without having to refer to the checklist.

Another interesting episode involved a whole team that was making too many mistakes.

A manager in a processing area had problems with the accuracy levels of the input staff. There were far too many errors, which caused time and effort in corrections and, if any were not detected in time, then customers would receive incorrect information in their bank statements.

He had to find a way of bringing the number of errors down to a minimum acceptable level but in a way that did not cause the staff to feel threatened or insecure.

After a great deal of thought, he came up with the idea of keeping a large chart on the wall that indicated who had committed how many errors each day.

"Ouch!" you may well start thinking. "This action would make the input clerks feel very exposed."

Actually, they found it fun. Why? It was the way in which the manager went about it. He discussed the error levels with the team and suggested to them that the chart be created and whoever made the most errors in a day would place a small (and very affordable) sum of money into a kitty. The kitty would then be used at the end of the week to buy biscuits for everyone's tea break on the Friday afternoon.

He also went on to say that, if the total number of errors in the week was below a certain figure (the minimum acceptable error level) he would foot the bill for the biscuits.

The idea was accepted and adopted by the team.

Within a few weeks, the team members took great delight in the fact that they were making sure he had to fork out for biscuits on every Friday afternoon!

I came across another, more difficult, situation that was handled in a very understanding way by a newly-appointed line manager.

Michael was a young, newly-promoted Supervisor in a bank. Together with other officers, one of his first duties of the day was to check the input clerk's work of the previous day. However, as the newest boy on the block, his initiation meant that he would now be responsible for reviewing the work of the worst input clerk of the lot. This clerk made a lot of errors, which made the Supervisor's work longer and more difficult.

On the very first day, when Michael returned the checked work to the clerk for correction, the clerk concerned said apologetically "because you are new, you have been given my work to check. I'm sorry, but I am not very good and I make lots of errors."

"Don't worry," replied Michael. "We all make mistakes. I am sure there will be fewer errors tomorrow."

The following day there were fewer mistakes. Michael made a point of mentioning it to the clerk and praising him for the improvement.

The next day there was a further reduction in errors, remarked upon by Michael saying "see? I knew things would improve."

The final result was that the clerk became not only the most accurate but also the quickest, making his name synonymous with quality, a reputation of which he was justly proud.

The general approach in all these real cases is similar — creating an environment in which people grow, thrive and go home at the end of the day with a degree of pride and excitement about what they have done, and where what they have done has been a very positive contribution to the workplace.

## Beware of achieving target!

We may set a goal of achieving no more than x or x% errors and be satisfied that we are keeping within this. However, we cannot afford to be satisfied. Why? For the simple reason that a "within target" level of errors may conceal a serious problem that is costing us dearly in one way or another.

When in a client company, I reviewed the performance measurements for errors in the typing pool. These revealed a very low margin of error of which they were justly proud. Their rate was 2% against the 5% maximum error standard set.

However, errors are a cost and, if improvement can be achieved with the minimum of bother, it can pay. I decided to dig deeper but when I asked for the records to commence a review and analysis of them, it caused consternation. In spite of my statements to the contrary, it was felt that we were doubting their competence, which was far from the truth.

My analysis showed that 7-10 rejections out of the 15-20 that happened each day were in one kind of letter only. It was an awkward letter because it was lengthy, full of detail, tabulated and had to be formatted every time.

On investigation, it was found that the major problem was the formatting. All other letters were pre-formatted as templates by the Supervisor and thus only required input of the variable information. This particular set of letters had not been formatted as templates and all the concentration on the intricate formatting caused errors in other input. In fact, the job was so tedious that only small batches of such letters were handled at a time by any one typist in order to maintain their sanity!

Realising the time, cost, and frustration that this was causing, the Supervisor immediately agreed to format the letter that day to standardise it. These specific frustrations and errors were soon a thing of the past and, as a further benefit, their quality standard was even better than before.

This live case study shows how even high standards can be improved, perhaps to everyone's benefit, if you are willing to analyse what is happening rather than just accept that things are going well.

### iii. Customer queries.

How can queries from our customers be a reflection on our quality?

The answer is simply that, if we are receiving similar queries from a number of customers about aspects of a certain product or service, we are increasing our non-productive workload. Each query has to be handled by someone and while this is being done, we cannot use that person's time to work on something that attracts income or adds value.

Another point is that it may well suggest we are not informing them well enough about the product or service and, if we proactively provide that information, the number of queries about it should diminish, reducing our costs accordingly. It will also cause less bother for the customer, ensuring our reputation is upheld.

It therefore makes sense to keep a record of customer enquiries and what they were about. This will enable us to monitor non-productive effort and, if we find some, we can set about planning ways of preventing it from continuing.

## *Conclusion.*

The kinds of data we need to collect are:

- Customer complaint details (from both internal and external customers)
- Details of errors that are made
- Details of customer queries.

The sort of detail we will need for analysing:

- Who was involved (not for chastising, but to determine of training/support is needed or a review of the system is required.)
- The date on which it occurred
- What went wrong
- How/why it went wrong

### 2.3.3. Revenues (Sales).

*SYNOPSIS:*

*Just as this element of business is as closely watched as Budget & Cost Control, there are also destructive short-term practices. These are highlighted in order to increase awareness of them.*

*As with earlier chapters, we discuss the data collection and points for analysis.*

-=-=-=-

Like costs, sales levels are usually a very closely monitored aspect of the business and one could conclude that there isn't much leeway for significant improvements. This is not necessarily the case.

I had little to do with sales whilst in change management but, on becoming a full-time consultant providing an excellent psychometric tool set, The McQuaig System™, I was much more involved because I was helping clients to increase their sales potential. This was done by ensuring clients focused on getting people with the natural behaviours that match those demanded by the role as well as ensuring they interview carefully on the additional, and the just as crucial, "learnt" behaviours.

From there, steadily delving deeper into the sales arena, I found there were definitely a lot more opportunities than one might expect. I also discovered people practices that were destroying, rather than building the potential for sales growth.

Starting with the non-people elements, what are the things we need to consider analysing? A few to review are below, some of which may possibly be taken into consideration already.

- Are some types of order more difficult or complex to fulfil? These may require more work than for other kinds of order and, unless differently priced, could in effect cause profit margins to be lower than we expect.

- Smaller orders are generally more expensive for us to supply. Are there market or customer segments that are mostly small orders, costing us more to satisfy?

- What are the real profit margins on different categories of customer?

- Do we get unjustified complaints from certain customers or customer types? Dealing with complaints is an additional cost factor and, when unjustified and relatively frequent, we need to re-think with whom we are willing to undertake business.

- Who are our difficult customers? For example, some agree specifications, price and delivery date and, once we set the wheels in motion, they suddenly want changes in specifications. We then have to stop the process in order to adjust, which might cause disruption not only on this order but also others that were due to follow for other customers. Especially if the same delivery date and pricing is also expected, this may be a signal to adjust pricing policy on such situations and/or whether we wish to retain their custom.

Some of the analysis for this will come from other sources (KRAs) like quality:

- complaints & errors = complexity of product = an expensive customer;
- volumes handled by customer category = processing costs = clarity of actual margins;

and so on.

These kinds of analyses will help us determine what type of customer we should be targeting and which to either charge more or refuse to work with.

You will notice that some of these items will potentially clash with the sales team's interests, which are to meet their sales targets and, no doubt, obtain their commission. This can lead to some strong differences of opinion, which leads us to the people element mentioned earlier.

One of the errors that is made is the incentives by way of commission.

You get what you pay for.

A double glazing company's representative rang our doorbell one evening.

"Good evening sir. I see you have had your windows replaced but I wonder whether you would like a quote for replacing your fascias and soffits?"

"No, thank you," I replied.

"Are you considering any home improvements in the near future?"

"Only a bathroom overhaul."

"We don't do bathrooms, but our quotes are valid for a year."

I said that the fascia work would not be considered for another 2-3 years.

"We guarantee the lowest prices and the quote won't cost you anything."

Again I emphasised my lack of interest.

"But it won't cost you a penny for a quote," he insisted. "It will give you an idea of costs and it will do me a favour as well."

"How will it do you a favour?" I asked, puzzled. "Do you get paid for each quote you obtain?"

"Yes."

I finally got him to leave.

Now let's consider the implications of this.

- A potential future customer feeling pressurised to take something he doesn't want, even if it is free. (I also made a note of the company's name to ensure I avoid them when the time came to consider the fascia work.)

- If I had agreed to the quote, the company would have to cover the cost of arranging for a person to visit us and spend time undertaking all the measurements around the house. Then sitting down to calculate and prepare a quote that will be need to be explained plus, of course, the time required in an effort to make the sale.

- And that is not all! They also have to reward my unwanted visitor for creating all this very expensive and wasted effort.

- I can only assume all these expenses are very carefully built into their pricing structure so the customers foot the bill in the end.

Think about it. If one quote in ten results in a sale, that poor purchaser is loaded with the cost of sales of all ten!

- And what value is the 10-year guarantee given by the company if it finally collapses under the weight of wasteful practices?

There is a powerful lesson to be learnt from all this and it relates to the reward structure. We will get what we pay for so we must be careful what we decide to reward. Reward for the number of quotes and we'll get quotes. Reward for leads, we'll get leads. Reward for quantity, we'll get quantity.

However as this case shows, we won't get what is not rewarded, such as quality or professional selling that leaves the customer knowing they have been helped to make a choice that is right for them. I certainly appreciate a salesperson who helps me in this way.

Misapplied incentives can work out far more expensive than we realise. Apart from the costs causing our competitiveness to go out of the window, we lose our reputation. People who have faced unprofessional selling do not hesitate to tell their friends (and anyone else who will listen) about the awful experience they had with our company.

Good reputations take a long time to build yet can be destroyed in the wink of an eye.

Another aspect of the people side of selling is that salespeople appear to have short lives. I do not mean this in the medical sense! I refer to the relatively high staff turnover that appears to occur within the sales teams.

Having seen quite a number of sales departments, I can understand why. Apart from the nature of salespeople themselves, there are a number of contributory factors from the management side that I refer to as the "Death Wish" because they appear to be trying to demoralise their direct reports in an effort to make them leave.

Two main factors are first: ineffective selection — taking people into sales roles to which they are not at all behaviourally suited. In an attempt to behave contrary to their nature all day, every day, they become unhappy, perhaps even stressed, and fail to perform. I find this to be even worse in the selection of commission-only sales people, who cost little and are quickly and easily dispensed with if they do not succeed.

The second is ineffective management of them. The wrong people are promoted or recruited into sales management.

These can be corrected/prevented and I have been involved in helping companies to do this but the subject is outside the scope of this book.

Let us therefore turn our attention to some of the other "Death Wish" activities of sales management.

Apart from creating ineffective — even damaging — "incentive schemes", a major performance deterrent is targets. Well, it is not so much targets themselves but more the way in which they are set.

> When talking to a Regional Sales Manager about targets, he happened to mention that he is given a target from the Head of Sales and, on splitting this amongst his Sales Managers, he takes the precaution of adding 10-15% to each. His logic was that, if he just handed on the actuals and they fell short in delivering, he would not meet his targets and would have to face the consequences. It therefore made sense to get them to aim higher and, if they fall short, they would hopefully still be within the prescribed numbers.

> I asked from where the Head of Sales got his targets. It was from the Board of Directors.

> "Do you think the Head of Sales adds a safety margin in a similar way when allocating targets to yourself and the other Regional Sales Managers?" I queried.

> "I know he does, but I don't know by what percentage," he replied.

> "And when the Sales Managers get their targets from you, would they be taking a similar precaution when allocating targets to the members of their teams?"

> "I believe so. It was certainly a common practice when I was at that level a few years back."

> "What happens if a salesperson does not hit target?"

> "We monitor this aspect closely because it is so important. In fact, their targets are broken down into monthly ones and, if they miss the target for the month, they are given a warning. Three misses and they are out. We replace them."

> "Let me see if I have understood," I continued. "The Head of Sales adds, say, 10% to the target given to you. You then add 10% of the 110% when allocating to your Sales Managers. Finally, the Sales Managers add 10% to the 121%."

> He nodded.

> "So the salesperson's target is overloaded by around 33% more than the company's and, if they fall short and only hit 100% of

the company's target, they are on a warning and could be sacked if that continues for another two months.

"First you push them for unrealistic goals, then sack them for achieving what the company actually wants.

"Have you ever wondered why the staff turnover in your salespeople is so high and why your Sales Managers are spending most of their time chasing up defaulters and in recruitment interviews rather than maybe adding sales of their own?"

"I never thought of it that way," was the candid response.

Another "Death Wish" action I found is that of giving everyone the same target, regardless of prior performance and, by the same token, increasing the target by a percentage of the previous year's target.

Let's assume that, for the coming year, the target is now last year's target (x) + 15%.

What does this mean to me as a salesperson?

If my achievement last year was x - 10% I am now faced with the prospect of having to increase my achievement by more than 25%. How can I possibly be expected to do this? Why give some impossible targets that make people feel defeated before they even start trying to sell?

In effect, companies are choosing to destroy people's morale, causing staff turnover and having to spend time recruiting replacements.

Generally speaking, surely, if we need sales to increase by 10%, we just need each salesperson to increase his or her own prior achievement by 10%.

Let us now stop and think about what we are trying to achieve here. We want to increase performance. How can we do this effectively? Like the main Chapter Heading says: by Ensuring Sixes are Scored.

By remembering to *"Lead from Behind"* and by using *"Ask! Don't tell!"*

Ensuring Sixes are Scored assisted one client company that listened to this argument. It was a very difficult assignment because the Regional Sales Managers whom I was training and coaching were petrified of losing control, such was the heavy emphasis on sales targets.

The first stage of the training was a discussion around what the preferred behaviours of a salesperson were and this, primarily, was a very strong goal-orientation and competitiveness, together with a fairly strong independence — they liked to make their own decisions as opposed to be told what to do, and even worse, how to do it.

I then asked how the sales targets were set for each individual. The answer? "We give it to them."

"So whose target is it?"

"Theirs, obviously."

"I suggest it is not their target. It is yours. They don't own it. Supposing we instead ask them what they want to set as their target for the coming year? After all, they like to make their own decisions and, once they have done this, they own it. It is theirs."

"We can't do that! It's too risky! Supposing they quote a figure that is well below what we need it to be? What do we do then? Do what we do now and give them the target they must reach?"

I then put forward the suggestion that they deal with this in exactly the same way as with someone who quotes such a high figure that is impossible to reach. This perplexed them. I therefore explained the process:

The answer is we say "O.K., so you want to hit that target. How do you plan to go about reaching it?" Then they outline their plan.

We question to get them to help them think things through. "Any other ways it can be done? What else would help make this work? What would prevent you from achieving what you want to achieve? How do you want to prevent that from happening or if it cannot be prevented, how do you want to lessen the negative impact on your achievements? What help do you need from me? ..."

If their plan makes sense, the potential pitfalls have been planned for, your help defined, then it should be committed to paper so we both have a reference point for the actions planned. We should also follow this up to make sure it is working for them and that we do not omit to provide the agreed support.

No doubt you will remember these points from both the Action Planning in Chapter 1.5 of this book and the "Ask! Don't tell!" principle. But this live case did not end there. It continued further.

The Regional Managers protested. "But that doesn't answer the question. If the person makes a plan to hit a target below what I need, how does that solve my problem? I have to ensure they reach the target I have been set!"

"If the plan makes sense and they undertake it, do you think they will try to beat their own target or just reach it?" I asked. "Remember, they are competitive people. All we are trying to do is to help people to be the best they can be. We want to help them be successful.

"Consider this. If a salesperson is not making the progress they want, we can sit down with them and ask them what is preventing them from reaching their goal and assist them to problem-solve. As Drucker says, we can help them "remove obstacles to performance." *(Op. cit.)*

Each of the Regional Managers decided to give this concept a try. I then spent time with each of them in turn to discuss each of their salespeople and how to approach them as individuals. We particularly focused on "problem people" and in questioning the manager on the situation, it was possible to diagnose the potential cause and set a way forward for dealing with it in a positive manner.

One month later, a review session took place. All reported a good degree of success: a greater rapport with their teams, stronger working relationships, greater understanding of their salespeople and one or two people who had not been performing too well had been 'turned around' and were progressing steadily.

I never cease to be amazed at what "Leading From Behind" can achieve.

### 2.3.4. Staff Morale.

*SYNOPSIS:*

*Even if using "Leading from behind" and "Ask! Don't tell!", there are some other important aspects of managing people that we must take into consideration and act upon.*

-=.-=.-=.-

As we have seen in preceding chapters, the morale of our team depends to a very great extent on the way we manage. If we have adopted the practice of "Leading From Behind", using "Ask! Don't Tell!" and further refining our skills with these tools as we learn from our experiences with them, then we are more likely to have a good morale level in our area.

However, there are other aspects that we need to consider in order to further support what we want to achieve with and for our team. We will take a look at a few of these.

## *Induction.*

When someone new joins the team, they are likely to feel a little uncomfortable. Everything is new to them. Everyone is new to them. It generally takes a while to settle. At the same time, if they are new recruits starting on probation, they are likely to be concerned about whether they will be good enough at their work to be kept on rather than terminated once the probation period is over.

Regardless of what HR department does (or does not do) we, as the new incumbent's manager, have to take active steps to help them in Scoring Sixes as quickly and as easily as possible. If we do this with them by using the action-planning process for learning, they will be able to set their targets and map their own progress in areas of importance to them and to their work. They can also request help where things are not working as well as they would like.

This approach can make things more straightforward for them. It can also mean we benefit from higher performance at an earlier stage. On top of this, it gets them used to our processes, open communications, and team approach to our work.

It is always wise to have an induction plan pre-prepared and involving members of the team in compiling this will be of great benefit for two reasons.

- First, especially from those who are relatively new, we will get closer to what would be very helpful for a newcomer.

- Second, helping a person fit into the team is best done by the team, not just us doing it by ourselves. For example, the newcomer may first spend some time getting to understand a little about the role they are to undertake.

Once they have begun to grasp this, it might help them see the bigger picture of where their role fits into the department's work. We can therefore get them to spend a little time with each team member to understand what they do and how.

Particularly if the team has come up with such an idea, they are likely to do this willingly and well whilst at the same time starting to create a bond between them and their new colleague.

A "buddy" approach could well prove helpful in providing a first point of contact for most of the routine issues: where the coffee machine is located, the washrooms, how the canteen operates, etc.

## *Development.*

We have spoken of ensuring we provide training to individuals who require it in order to achieve what they want to achieve. This is in fact one arena in which things can falter. Even though we may strongly recommend training for a person, HR department may not have a sufficient enough demand to be able to provide an in-house course. There may not be external providers or placements available. Many managers unfortunately take the approach of explaining the situation to their team member and then shrugging their shoulders and saying they did their best but it is out of their hands and no more can be done.

This does not help the individual and it does not help our results. It is also likely to erode his/her morale and could even undermine the rapport we have so far managed to build.

Instead, a far more constructive activity will be to start a problem solving session together.

*"If you want to solve problems you should imagine the solution beyond the obstacles; if the obstacles capture your full attention, you may get stuck there forever"* ~ Ioannis Gousgounis

Heeding Ioannis Gousgounis' suggestion, we can start a conversation something like the following.

"Unfortunately, HR is unable to assist with the training you need, so let's put our heads together to see how we can find a way of ensuring you get what is essential for you to accomplish your goal. First, let's define the critical learnings, and then we can brainstorm to see what ideas we can think of for obtaining it from elsewhere."

More often than not, there are viable alternatives. Who was doing this kind of work earlier and might be able to impart the knowledge? Are there any books or other publications that might help? Could a search on the Internet throw some light on the subject? Of course there is also the real potential that we ourselves can impart the training needed.

> I recall being in this kind of situation, where most of the staff in my unit were not undertaking a certain type of process correctly and opening up far too many avenues for audit problems. It had to be changed but training was not available from anywhere because we were in an isolated small town and almost a day's travel from the central office where the training centre was located.
>
> There was but one option left. On a day that was less busy, the word was put out to all staff, requesting them to try to complete their work 30 minutes early so we could have a training session. They did so.
>
> With a makeshift flip chart, I took them through the major security measures that were important in this work, what we were required to do and also the reasons for this. This was the first time anyone had bothered to impart a training session in the unit and the questions flew thick and fast.
>
> When we reached their "end of day", I called a halt to the questions and said it was now time for them to leave. They remonstrated with me, saying they had more questions to be

answered. I pointed out that I could only expect them to remain in office until 5.00pm, no overtime was allowed, so it would not be fair to retain them after that hour.

To my amazement, they argued. They were not interested in overtime. They wanted their questions answered. I refused on principle, and they argued more. I looked at the Union representative and he merely smiled and said "no issues. Please answer their questions. Forget overtime."

So we continued for another 15 minutes or so.

The result was that the kinds of errors that had been so numerous earlier became the exception rather than the rule.

Because of the extremely positive response, I suggested to one of the senior members of staff, who was comfortable with public speaking, that he pick up a subject he felt people would enjoy learning about and we could repeat the exercise. This was also well received by both him and the staff.

## Cross-training.

Many managers take over a team and continue from there without assessing the skills, knowledge and experience of each person reporting to them. There are some important questions to be asked.

### How long has each person been in the role they are currently performing?

Hopefully, you will not find someone has been in the job for 27 years like the fellow I mentioned in Part 1 but we must also avoid the strong temptation of keeping someone trapped in a job because they are good at it and a replacement will be hard to find and/or because of the time it will take to train someone to the same level of performance.

We cannot make a hard and fast rule about the length of time a person should hold a certain post. The reason I say this is that some people enjoy fairly regular change while others prefer a degree of stability and like to build and maintain a routine that runs like clockwork.

We need to be alive to giving individuals something new to learn, something new to do, so their knowledge and skills are increased and they do not feel stuck in a rut. Building and maintaining a chart that shows us what they have already learnt and, if possible, the level of skill they have built in each role will enable us to plan job rotation. It will be positive if a person can move from the most simple towards the most complex over a period of time — they will see they are progressing.

Apart from imparting greater skills and knowledge to our team members and adding to their value, this exercise also enables us to have an internal support structure for when someone takes leave. We have others who can immediately step in to help keep that person's work under control with very little or no training time needed to get them up to speed.

**Whom should we be grooming for what kind of future role?**

Most managers seem to think that "grooming" means preparing someone to be a manager. We should not fall into this trap. Some may well have innate leadership strengths: seeing the big picture, setting direction, ready to make decisions and take responsibility for them — and not just the "technical" decisions but more far-reaching ones. They are less comfortable with detail and they use initiative. People of this nature are generally more likely to take the management mantle comfortably.

The experts, the ones who are excellent with detail, are a "safe pair of hands" and risk-averse, are less likely to be comfortable with decisions outside their area of expertise. Here are the ones to groom towards greater and greater in-depth knowledge and expertise because they like to become the "fount of all knowledge" to whom everyone can turn for information and support on their topic. This is much more appealing to them than worrying about what others are doing or not doing.

For "manager" types, we can consider giving them responsibilities of a general nature (as opposed to tasks) and perhaps get them to undertake a degree of supervision, such as with a small project. Most importantly, we must be prepared to coach them because it is important they do not start building the kinds of habits that are detrimental for the business and for those they are learning to lead. We must guide them in "Leading from behind" and in how they can use "Ask! Don't tell!" to achieve it.

For the "expert" individuals, we should be on the look-out for jobs that test their expertise and provide the opportunity to learn more in order to accomplish the task. Ever more complex problems will be likely to provide them plenty of opportunity to grow in the direction they enjoy.

Whatever the plan is for helping them develop, it should be "formalised" into an Action Plan with the various milestones of learning clarified so they can review their progress and ensure they are reaching their goal, as we saw a little earlier in this section.

I must admit I obtain a total advantage by using The McQuaig System™ because it clearly states how a person best learns and also the kind of role in which they are likely to thrive. The System also identifies morale level and, if low morale is evident, it provides clues about the potential causes. This makes it much simpler to diagnose the real cause and set about correcting it.

The most prevalent causes are wrong placement of a person and/or ineffectual management of them. The corrective action normally brings a significant improvement in both morale and performance.

For these reasons, I have generally advised my clients to build the assessments into the appraisal process and this has proved highly productive.

There is another vital measurement that we need to make, which is:

## Staff turnover/attrition.

People leave a company and move on. It is a fact of life but there are some ramifications behind this. The cost factor of recruiting a replacement, training them in and waiting for them to become effective can be quite substantial. On top of these costs are those of the outgoing individual potentially performing less well, perhaps complaining to colleagues on our team and thereby possibly indirectly prompting them to follow suit.

If we can get an idea of these costs, we will get a picture of how it is affecting our budget. I normally try to get managers and HR people to realise the true implications of staff turnover by asking them to undertake a couple of calculations:

- What is the company's annual profit before tax as a percentage of sales?

- Using that percentage, calculate how much product we need to sell just to pay for the staff attrition.

The answer can be quite alarming.

This often draws a relatively straight line from morale to profits: our KRA of Budget and Cost Control.

So what causes people to decide to leave us? Some prime reasons are:

- Being in a job they don't enjoy.

- Being managed in a manner that is incompatible to their nature.

- Not having the opportunity to grow and develop in a way that is right for them.

If it is any of these factors, we have to urgently and effectively re-think what we are doing because the odds are that the situation has occurred because of us.

However, if we have followed "Leading From Behind", used the "Ask! Don't tell!" approach and included questions on their developmental needs and aspirations, particularly when working on action planning with them, we are likely to be given relevant information by each individual.

It is then up to us to work accordingly. (The two case studies at the end of Chapter 1.3.1. "Performance Management? No! Lead From Behind instead" illustrate this in action.)

## 2.3.5. Timeliness (of delivering products/services).

*SYNOPSIS:*

*If processes take too long to undertake, they not only affect our delivery to the customers but also cause unnecessary costs.*

*We study what data should be collected and analysed and what misunderstandings we need to avoid.*

*The subject of time management also fits under this heading, so we take a brief look at how we can analyse our use of time.*

-=-=-=-

*Time is a crucial indicator because it provides strong clues of lost potential.*

Ensuring prompt and on-time product or service delivery is important. Late deliveries do nothing for our reputation for reliability, and definitely give our competitors an opportunity to serve our customers better — and forever.

In today's markets, this aspect of our work is under constant pressure. People seem to be in a permanent "I want it now!" mode. An example will be where our customer is running a "Just In Time" process. Prompt delivery — even at short notice — can be a demand we will have to face on a regular basis.

But there is more to this than our service to our customers, be they internal or external. If we are slow to complete something, it is quite possible that we have a process that is time-consuming and, therefore, expensive. This would impact our costs, our pricing and our profit margins. In turn, this too affects our competitiveness.

As was mentioned in a previous chapter, Budget & Cost Control, ineffectual managers tend to resort to staffing their area to cope with the periods of peak loads and, as a result have idle time that is merely wasting resources. It is therefore a delicate balance that has to be struck to ensure timely delivery without undue expense. As a result, the kinds of approach to staff costing mentioned in the Budget chapter will necessarily apply here. We must also remember to ...

## *Keep targets reasonable.*

Although it is nice to see people getting a buzz out of creating improvements, we must ensure they remain objective. People tend to want to achieve even better results in a situation they have already improved. They want to make it better still. Great sentiments, but what would be the outcome?

> A manager of a fairly large department in the bank had set his sights on making the encashment of a cheque a much quicker process in order to be competitive and to create more customer satisfaction. After executing the plan he had devised, the time it took was successfully brought down from 15 minutes to just five. We were "celebrating" his success, of which he was justly proud, when he announced he now wanted to set a new target of three minutes.
>
> "A laudable target," I said to him. "But what are our competitors achieving at the moment?"
>
> "8 — 10 minutes," he replied.
>
> "We are well ahead of the competition, so will that two minutes make that big a difference? On top of that, how much effort will be needed to shave that time off of your service? Will it mean additional staff, less focus on other things that need to be done, pushing people to work too fast, maybe introducing errors in the rush?"
>
> He frowned as he thought things through. "No," he finally answered. "The disadvantages will probably outweigh the advantages. It would put too much pressure on us and I think I should focus on another area of improvement instead."

This underlines the need for us to carefully keep things in balance.

## *What should we measure?*

It becomes very important to know where we stand in terms of our timeliness standards so that we can make informed judgements rather than assuming everything seems OK. This does mean we need to collect and collate the facts. One way of creating useful data for analysis is first to make a list of every kind of item processed in our area then, on a daily basis:

- Record the time of each item's entry into our area.

- The time it is released as complete by us.

- The number of such items processed, by day, week, and month.

Collecting such information for at least a month will allow us to question the data.

- Is our timeliness standard for this kind of item competitive (whether for an external customer or an internal one)?

- What timeliness standard should we be aiming for?

- Why does it take this long?

- How can it be processed differently/more quickly?

- Why does it take just as long to process a batch of 20 items as it does to process 30?

We must also bear in mind where we belong in the process and what else is involved prior to or post our part in it. In other words, we may feel that our processing is timely but, when we consider what has to be undertaken before and/or after our work, what is the final result for the "end user"?

For example, we may consider that completing our work on an item and handing it over for dispatch at 5.30pm is a job well done. However, Dispatch cannot deal with it today because 5.30pm is end of day and people are going home. It therefore gets sent the following day. The result? It takes an extra day to reach the customer.

It is possible to dig even deeper. Just one addition to the timeliness sheet could be the number of unprocessed items carried over to the next day. We have to be careful here. It is wise to "age" the items carried over:

- "0" refers to items received today,

- "+1" are items received yesterday that we have still not managed to process today,

- "+2" for items received the day before yesterday and still outstanding

- "+3" for those from the previous day.

More may be required, depending upon our situation.

On carrying the outstanding items forward to the following day, they are entered on that day's timeliness sheet as plus one, so items received yesterday and not processed yesterday are brought forward as "+1", not "0". The same increment applies to other, older, items brought forward.

This enables us to get an even clearer picture of the timeliness of our processing and help us focus on why things are carried forward and work on a way to limit the number of items being delayed. Naturally, it also helps us identify priorities — those items that are long outstanding need our more urgent attention.

The results will obviously need reviewing on a regular basis — perhaps month-ends — although some of your direct reports may well realise for themselves that more urgent action needs to be taken, and take it. We must remember to deal with shortfalls with care if we want our direct reports to remain in high morale-high performance mode. Let's take a look at a live case from my days in banking.

## *How failure to meet timeliness standards can be mismanaged.*

The General Manager of an area comprising about a dozen branches of a bank was facing a dilemma. The Central Bank of the country demanded certain reports to be sent to them on a regular basis each month. On average, 5 different reports were required each month. However, all branches delivered them late and this incurred fines from the Central Bank on a *per diem* basis.

The fines were averaging 7 days per return. Thus 12 branches, submitting five returns per month, all seven days late, incurred total fines of £10,000 equivalent per annum. To eradicate this would therefore add a straight £10,000 to profits.

(Please note: £10k at the time of this incident a couple of decades or so ago is considerably more in "today's" money!)

Something had to be done, so the General Manager issued circulars to remind branches of the need to get the returns submitted well on time.

Nothing changed.

He then issued letters to branch managers to bring this to their notice more forcibly.

Nothing changed.

He finally issued letters telling the branch managers that they were going to be held personally responsible for the failings of their branches.

Still nothing changed. Totally frustrated by the lack of responsibility of his branch managers, the General Manager did not know what to do next. He brought the subject out into the open with me. What kind of disciplinary action would best suit the situation?

I proceeded to take the General Manager through a problem solving process.

"What is the reason for the returns being delayed?" I asked.

"The branch managers are not effective enough."

"Why are they ineffective? Have you asked them why they are not complying with the Central Bank requirements?"

"Yes."

"What reasons do they give?"

"They are short staffed and the machines keep breaking down," he replied.

"Let's leave the staffing issue for the moment and look at the machinery. How many branches have this problem and how often?"

"They all face it, and quite regularly."

"Is this a fact or fabrication?"

"Yes, it is true. In fact, as a result, they have to do more work manually and that is partly why they find themselves short-staffed."

"How old are the machines?"

"About one year."

"And they are breaking down regularly?"

"Yes."

I was rather surprised by this, so enquired "if the machines are only about 12 months old, surely they should not be causing so much trouble. Has a complaint been made to the suppliers?"

"Yes, the branch managers have all complained individually."

"What has transpired?"

"They have been referred to the maintenance company."

"Are the machines regularly serviced, then?"

"Yes, they are. However, it appears that the company, which makes its money by servicing and repairs of this brand of machine, deliberately ensure that they have to be called out again and again so that they can earn more."

"Is that a fact?"

"It certainly appears to be."

"What has been done about that?"

"Branch managers have complained to the servicing management in their areas."

"And what happened?"

"Nothing."

"So, branch manager complaining to branch manager is not working. What else has been done?"

"Nothing."

"Where is the Head Office of this maintenance company?"

"In the capital city of the country."

"Where are you based?"

"In the capital."

"Have you tried a General Manager to General Manager complaint?"

"No."

"Would such a complaint carry more weight that a branch manager to branch manager one?"

"Yes ... Yes. I will take that action and, if it does not work, go higher up the ladder."

"And if that achieves nothing?"

"There's nothing much else that can be done."

"How much income does that maintenance company make from their franchise?"

"They are doing well."

"So, if they lost the franchise ...?"

"You mean complain about them to their principals, the machine manufacturers?"

"Yes."

"I think I had better do something about that too."

I then reverted to the staff aspect with one last, rather pointed, question. "What is the point in starting disciplinary action against your branch managers for action that could only be successfully undertaken at Head Office level?"

There was no answer given to this, just a worriedly apologetic frown.

As you can see, instead of using the lack of adherence to standards as a signal to investigate reasons, commands were issued that only produced undue pressures and fear. When "Ask! Don't tell!" was applied, the true causes were brought to light to be dealt with by the appropriate level of authority.

Talking of levels of authority reminds me of another timeliness issue I encountered when undertaking productivity missions where the timeliness standards reported showed an unduly long average wait that customers faced when encashing a cheque at the bank's counter.

Investigating the process showed it appeared to follow the usual practice: the technical aspects of the cheque are checked (e.g. words and figures agree), then the signature is validated. Finally the balance on the account checked and, if all was well, the payment was made.

This does not appear too lengthy. Time to dig deeper. I asked who authorises the cheque for payment. The response was that there were different levels of authority depending upon the value of the instrument. This was a quite normal part of such processes but I asked for the authority list and it seemed to contain nothing out of the ordinary. It was something like:

Up to £50 by the Head Clerk of Current Accounts.

£51 - £100 by the Manager of Current Accounts.

£101 - £500 by the Assistant Manager - Operations.

£501 - £5,000 by the Operations Manager.

£10,000+ by the Branch Manager.

I then asked one of my trademark "stupid" questions. "So, if the cheque is for £550, once the Head Clerk has checked all the technical aspects, the signature and the balance, he or she gives it to the Operations Manager?"

"No. It goes to the Manager of Current Accounts."

"What does he do?"

"He checks the technical aspects, the signature and balance and initials the instrument to show he has done this."

"So he then hands it to the Operations Manager."

"No. He hands it to the Assistant Manager - Operations."

"What does he do?"

"He checks the technical aspects, the signature and balance and initials the instrument to show he has done this."

... We will stop the process description there to keep it short but the cheque would be checked by each of the tiers in the authorities list until it finally reaches the appropriate one, who would also undertake the same checks before authorising payment.

It didn't take long to get the process changed to have the cheque routed directly from the cashier to the appropriate authorising signatory and the average time for cheque encashment dropped considerably.


*But where is the time to think about timeliness?*


One problem faced by many managers is, being under so much pressure to deliver, there is hardly any time to think and analyse what we are doing and how we are doing it. The focus is getting the product out of the door on time. If it is a more constant pressure, then we are likely to be forever fire-fighting rather than sitting back and questioning our organisation and processes.

Many managers face this difficulty, particularly the small/medium business owner/manager.

One major issue is really due to the results of several others: there always seem to be 1,001 things to sort out as far as operations are concerned. As a result, it becomes very difficult to find the time to focus on the "big picture" and to lead the organisation forward.

Why is this? What are some of the underlying situations that create it?

Senior managers or owner/directors often find it difficult, if not impossible, to rely on their subordinate managers to deal with things on their own because too many of them resort to procrastination rather than dealing with situations head-on. Alternatively, decisions are made that just do not make sense and can actually make things worse rather than better. Failing either of these, some managers will refer every single thing for decision, however minor, instead of making the decision themselves within their authority level.

Particularly in India, I found that problems, sometimes significant ones, are "kept under the carpet", hidden away. I can only surmise this is either in the vain hope that the boss will not notice or that the issue will somehow sort itself out if we wait long enough. Of course, neither of these wishes is generally granted and the boss is now forced to wade in, take personal command, and spend time to get things sorted out at "shop floor" level.

From these kinds of situation, the Senior Manager learns to keep a constant watchful eye on everyone and on everything that is happening — or not happening — so they can catch the problems early and solve them before it is too late. The larger the organisation, the greater the time needed to monitor and manage it properly to ensure quality and delivery schedules are met and there are no cost overruns. Customers have to be satisfied and profits need to be made.

We can understand their feeling of being trapped in a never-ending circle of fire-fighting just to keep the business on its feet, let alone trying to build it into something bigger and better.

In effect, the owner is managing almost everything because the managers aren't managing. Due to the constant pressures, owners are unable to find the time to think more deeply and broadly about solutions that can, and will, make significant changes for the better.

*Is there a cure?*

To help such managers regain control over the situation (and as a further result in some cases, also regain their personal lives), I have persuaded them to keep a Time Sheet (see the next page for a sample). The rules for completing this format are simple but strict discipline is needed to ensure we optimise the potential benefits:

- Print off some copies and keep them in a clipboard (or ring binder) so you can quickly access them to make brief notes as the day goes on.

- Carry it with you and keep it updated as you go.

- Do not leave it to the end of the day to construct it from memory. This will lose potentially valuable data.

- A separate sheet (or set of sheets) for each day.

- Keep notes brief but clear & concise.

- Complete a set for at least a week, preferably two weeks.

**Figure 3. Sample Time Sheet Format.**

| TIME SHEET | NAME: | | | DAY: | | | | | DATE: |
|---|---|---|---|---|---|---|---|---|---|

| From Time | To Time | Time Spent | Activity | With Whom | Rvnu | Cntrl | Cost | Qual | Time | Staff Sat | Other | Result / Achievement / Outcome / Notes |
|---|---|---|---|---|---|---|---|---|---|---|---|---|
| | | | | | | | | | | | | |
| | | | | | | | | | | | | |
| | | | | | | | | | | | | |
| | | | | | | | | | | | | |
| | | | | | | | | | | | | |
| | | | | | | | | | | | | |
| | | | | | | | | | | | | |
| | | | | | | | | | | | | |
| | | | | | | | | | | | | |
| | | | | | | | | | | | | |

113

## Notes on completing the Time Sheet:

- "From-To" columns are for the timings of the activity.

- "With whom": all those who are involved in the activity with you. (We must remember that, while people are with us, they cannot focus on their own work. It is therefore important to ensure the discussion is pertinent to them.)

- The columns with the KRA areas only need to be ticked as appropriate to each activity.

- The final column is important - note what resulted from the activity and any thoughts you have about it.

Once the 1-2 weeks' data has been entered, you can then sit down and analyse what is taking what amount of your time and how much each focuses on your main KRAs.

## There are many questions to be asked. A few are:

- When are the most frequent interruptions I get?

- Am I trying to undertake longer tasks or strategic thinking during the times of frequent interruptions instead of when things tend to be quieter?

- Whose work am I doing and how much time am I spending on their tasks?

- Am I doing things that do not need to be done?

- Am I delegating sufficiently? If not, why not? What do I need to do about it?

To underline the utility and potential of this exercise, one client who undertook this fairly recently advised me it helped him realise where some time & effort was being lost. He changed the way he undertook an activity, resulting in something like a 70% enhancement to that area of his work.

Even more recently, another client obtained the stark reality of where his efforts were going and, after discussion with me, saw clearly why this was happening. It resulted in some difficult but important decisions being made and executed, releasing him from a significant amount of work. This enabled him to focus on expansion plans and, I dare add, made him a more relaxed and happy person.

## *Conclusion.*

We need to measure how we use our time and the extent to which the usage focuses on the priorities of our KRAs.

We also need to log details of volumes as mentioned above.

Analysis of the data in a manner suggested should provide the clues for potential improvement of our results under this KRA. This process again demands we consider the aspects we looked at in 2.3.1. Budget & Cost Control:

- Who is doing what?
- Why are they doing it?
- How are they doing it?
- When are they doing it?

As you can see, the volume data and analysis supports our approach to two or three KRAs, which is indeed very helpful — killing three birds with one stone ... well, to an extent at least!

## 2.4. Building further on the strengths of the "Ask! Don't tell!" concept.

*SYNOPSIS:*

*"Ask!Don't tell!" is a powerful, positive, interpersonal aid to many situations both at work and outside it.*

*We now look at a few ways in which it can add great value to activities such as coaching individuals and also problem solving — even in a team environment. As usual, some pertinent live cases are used to illustrate how it can work.*

-=-=-=-

We saw in the earlier part of this book that this concept gives us a strong edge in Pioneering Powerful Performance, increasing morale, engagement and results.

What I have found is the "Ask! Don't tell!" approach is extremely versatile and can be used for interaction with people on a day-to-day basis, including non-work situations. It is also a very useful tool for coaching because it helps the individual think things through more carefully and more fully.

"I am having a serious problem with a colleague," stated a manager. "I think he is trying to make me look bad for his own political reasons. How do I deal with this?"

"Can you give me an example so I can understand the situation more clearly?"

"Yes. When I need something done by his department in order to complete my tasks and meet my deadlines, he says he is too busy to accept it or takes it and doesn't complete within the time I need it. I end up not delivering and have to take the rap when it is not my fault — it's his."

"I can see what you mean. It must be very difficult to contend with. Why do you say it is for his own political reasons?"

"Why else would he do this to me?"

"That is an interesting question. Will you do something for me?"

"Yes, sure. What is it?"

"On your notepad, please jot down ten possible reasons why your colleague might be doing this."

About eight items were listed and the manager said he couldn't think of any more. I asked him to read them out.

Interestingly, the first 3-4 were quite negative about the colleague but, after that, some more "understanding" possibilities followed.

"Thank you. Now you have listed all those as *possibilities*, the first is the one you mentioned as the actual reason. Why did you discount all the others when you made that initial decision that number one was the reason?"

"Well, to tell the truth, I never thought about any others at the time."

"What you have done is unfortunately a normal human trait. We tend to jump to a conclusion about the motive behind what someone has said or done and that motive is most often a negative one. We all tend to do it. So what I would like you to do now is think about the other items on your list and see what you think might really be behind your colleague's behaviour."

After a few minutes' thought, he replied. "I think it is number seven. The pressures he is under. Thinking again, he does have some tight deadlines himself and it must be difficult for him to drop everything to meet my demands."

"How certain are you about that?"

"Very."

"OK, feel free to check it out with him to validate but for now let's work on the assumption that you have hit the right nail on the head. How do you think you could make it easier for him to help you in future?"

"Perhaps I could speak to him as soon as I know that help is needed by me and see if he can plan ahead to release some time for my work. Thinking about it, I do tend to leave it to the last moment rather than speak to him as soon as I know his help is required. That must make it difficult for him. I could even ask him the question you have asked me — how I can help him to help me."

This is not all. One of the most difficult situations is dealing with the dispirited, even angry, employee. This is especially so when they feel they have been wrongly judged. Here is a real situation that demonstrates how asking, not telling, defused a rather tense situation and was another milestone in my learning. It occurred when I was conducting a bank audit in a branch unit.

> When the bank closed its doors behind the last customer of the day, there was a sudden eruption of angry voices among the counter service staff. It grew in intensity and was quite disturbing. However, the branch manager remained seated in his cabin even though the door was wide open and he would have heard the *fracas*.

> The manager was an extremely nice person but, I realised, one who did not like dealing with confrontation. Yet something needed to be done. Although it was not within my remit, I walked over to the centre of the storm and said "you all seem very upset about something. Would you mind if I asked what the problem is?"

> One of the most angry-looking clerks replied forcibly "I will certainly tell you what the problem is. I have been turned down for promotion again!"

> Before I could say anything more, he blurted on: "Management have their favourites, their "blue-eyed boys". Just because I was a Union Leader, they have it against me!"

> He continued on for a while about the reasons and motives behind his being denied a promotion.

> This brought a roar of support from the rest of the people, who then began vociferously adding their comments about the unfairness meted out to this individual.

> "I am sorry to hear you feel that way about it," I ventured. "Obviously, I cannot talk for local management decisions because I am not attached to this region. However, if you wish, I will be happy to discuss things further with you."

> This offer brought consent.

> "You have some strong views about how the decision was made and how the wrong criteria were used in your case. Would you mind if I asked you a question?"

> "Sure, go ahead."

> "Supposing you were responsible for making decisions on promotions, what would be the criteria you would use?"

The clerk rapidly listed 9-10 qualities, none of which could I disagree with and I said so. I then asked if he would write this list on a sheet of paper, which he did.

"Would you be willing to look at each of these items you have listed and rank yourself against each one: 0 if you have little or no experience, knowledge or skills in that area, and up to 10, where you are really great at it?"

He shrugged his shoulders. "Why not," he replied and set about the task.

When he had finished, I pointed out that the list was personal to him and I did not expect him to share the contents with me if he didn't want to. I then asked if there were any qualities that he had given very low scores.

He marked three items, turned the page around for me to see, and said "yes. Those three."

"Do you think it possible that one, or even all of those, could have let you down in the promotion?"

He thought seriously for a moment, then looked me straight in the eyes and said "yes, all of them."

"Do you still want to be a manager?" I then asked.

"Definitely."

"So, when the next promotion round takes place, do you want these three items to stand in your way?"

"No, I don't."

"In that case, what do you think you can do to strengthen these areas so that they don't let you down next time?"

The clerk then started discussing and formulating plans for making his position stronger for the next opportunity.

The clerk's shift from a strong and negative indignation to planning how he can improve his prospects not only defused the situation but also brought positivity. Had I been his manager, I would have asked about what support he needed from me to help him and then followed it through.

This is a complete contrast to the often-heard "I am sorry to hear you weren't selected. Unfortunately, I had no part in the decision-making but I did recommend you." In other words, "please sir, it wasn't me - it was him!" (And I hang my head in shame for also having employed such useless "placations" occasionally, prior to this event.)

Again, yet another piece of learning in a different direction stemmed from this incident. When the clerk focused on what he wanted, he was more than ready to draw up and embark on a series of actions to achieve his goal. In other words, he was motivated. Generally, when people really want something, they are more than willing to do something about it. If I, as his manager, try to motivate him by telling him what he should aim for and what he should do about it, it would get neither of us anywhere. It has to be what he wants, not what I think he should want.

Once you get to understand where a person wants to be, what they want to achieve and what they enjoy immensely, we know what motivates them. All we have to do is help them find relevant and helpful experiences in the work they do with us.

Too idealistic? Too far from the real world? No! It *is* the real world!

Sometimes it may mean you help that person gain the skills and knowledge to move to another company that will fulfil their ambitions better than we can. Is this not far better than keeping them trapped in unfulfilling work that will only serve to demotivate a person so they lose that inner spark? They suffer, their work is just about OK rather than outstanding, they lose, the company loses and so do we because we are not achieving as much as we could from the team.

Let us now move forward to the next section to see another potent use of this concept.

### 2.4.1. Problem Solving In A Team Environment: *The Problem Solving Workshop.*

*SYNOPSIS:*

*Based on both "Leading from Behind" and "Ask! Don't tell!", this chapter lays the foundation — a process — for great team work.*

*Not only that, it helps identify "hidden" problems and opportunities.*

*It is so powerful that it has even found solutions for problems previously considered "unsolvable".*

.=.=.=.

In the previous part of the book, I mentioned how a General Manager - IT used "Ask! Don't tell!" to drive a major project with his team, gaining their total commitment. This is actually an idea I had much earlier experimented with when in Management Development in an International Training Centre: The Problem Solving Workshop. Let's take a closer and deeper look at this very powerful method of working with people, whether in a discrete team or a cross-functional one.

Problems happen. They are a fact of life and certainly a fact of working life. A large number of people believe it negative to speak of "problems" and insist we use the word "challenge" instead. Strange, but true. My own personal viewpoint is that it matters little. Whatever you want to call it, so long as we see it, it means the same thing: we need to find a way of removing it.

Why did I use the phrase *"so long as we see it"*?

It never ceases to amaze me that there are so many problems that we just do not see. We are blind to them so they become "hidden problems". The question that naturally follows is "why don't we see them?" The answer is: because we no longer look for them.

An example is something that perhaps wastes time yet we continue to do what has been done before because that is what we have been told to do or "nothing can be done about it", so we just have to live with it. Nobody questions the existence of this anymore — it is a part of the regular landscape to the point of being invisible. Let me cite an example of this blindness but in a different context.

In my younger years, our family lived in the County Town of Kent: Maidstone. One summer, we had a Belgian couple staying with us for a week or two and, when I returned from college one Friday afternoon, our friends waxed eloquent about the beauty of the town centre. I laughed and commented that it wasn't at all beautiful.

"But there are lovely flowers hanging in baskets on the lamp-posts and ..."

"There aren't any flowers hanging from lamp-posts," I interrupted.

My father, who was listening to this exchange, smiled at me and said "next time you go into town, just have a look and see for yourself."

The next morning, I had to go into the town and, once there, I stopped and made a point of looking at the main street. It was an eye-opener! The town centre was in fact rather picturesque with a number of very old buildings and — you'd never guess — there certainly were baskets of pretty flowers hanging from the lamp-posts.

I had been into the town hundreds of times but, because I was there so often, I no longer looked. I no longer saw. As the old saying goes, "familiarity breeds contempt."

This is one of the main reasons I have found for the existence of the "hidden problems" lurking quietly and totally undisturbed while they drain some of the valuable lifeblood out of the organisation and weaken its performance and potential.

It is therefore important to identify these "hidden problems", drag them into the open, and subject them to a process that will kill them off completely or at least lessen their impact significantly.

However, when I first started Pioneering Powerful Performance, I found there were so many visible problems to solve that the "hidden" ones got placed on the back burner for a while. The only drawback in doing this might be one or two of them may well be making it more difficult to deal with the apparently more important/urgent ones. The Problem Solving Workshop process we are about to look at will take this into account to some degree.

## *The origins of The Problem Solving Workshop.*

In the early 1980s while working with an international bank, I was transferred to the International Training Centre in Bombay (now called Mumbai), the financial hub of India. My main thrust was in the area of management because I had recognised this as an area that needed a sea change from the then current "command and control" approach partly driven, I think, by the natural fear managers had of what appears to be a "letting go" of their control over people and events. The results were naturally less than optimum performance. I firmly believed we needed to change our style to be able to enhance morale and performance.

This is, of course, a phenomenon that is found in many companies: it is not peculiar to that one organisation. It is a culture that easily leads to problems being kept hidden from the boss in order to secure self-preservation. Problems, however, like many plants, grow almost uncontrollably in the dark, to the extent that they cause more damage than they would have if brought into the open at an early stage and nipped in the bud.

There were a couple of "Management Development" courses in existence but, after running them a few times, I realised that, although filled with "good stuff", they were to a great extent theoretical. The big question in my mind was how many of the participants passing through our centre would be able to "translate" motivational theory into 'this is what I need to do with this "problem" person, in my area and undertaking this kind of work, in order to turn things around to make them a more positive contributor'?

Unless participating managers went back to their desks and started to do things differently and more effectively, the days spent in the training room were tantamount to useless. An interesting time spent, meeting new people, having great food, and a welcome change from day-to-day work is all very well but, surely, the objective should also be to make a significant positive impact on the morale and results of their teams?

Although my performance was measured on the basis of the development of modules on new topics, running the requisite number of courses and the scores on participant feedback sheets, I adopted one of making the programmes more practical and usable in order to make a real difference to line managers' results. To this end, I started a total revision of everything but was still not satisfied that it was creating enough impact.

Trying to marry the subject of problem solving with a different leadership style brought a series of questions to my mind:

- how do we encourage people to fearlessly bring their problems out into the open before they appear to be getting a little out of hand?

- How do we ensure managers treat the problems objectively instead of blaming their subordinate for the trouble caused?

- How do we help managers realise the potential synergy in group problem solving techniques so that they would try to utilise and benefit from them?

- This naturally leads to the tough issue of: how can we prove that such techniques really work?

- Can we also manage to build an approach that will also demonstrate the team spirit that can be built from such joint exercises and thus open eyes and minds to the benefits of a Theory Y form of management?

It was when I was trying to find a practical way of dealing with this that I realised we could use real live problems in place of off-the-shelf case studies. By getting the participants to bring a live issue they were actually facing and needing to solve, we would not only be demonstrating a process but also solving some real problems. The fact that these would be the proverbial "boil on the backside" for a manager would mean they would be far more likely to attempt a worthwhile solution. We would be turning theory into practice and, hopefully, illustrating to the managers how they can do this with their teams.

The subject took on a whole new light. From good old solid "Problem Solving", it turned into "Problem Solving in a Team Environment".

It also meant I had to do a good deal of further research so I devoured books, articles and anything else I could find on the subject. From this, I pieced together an approach, a process, that I thought would have an impact.

When the next management development course was announced and nominations made, I sent instructions to all participants that they must bring with them a very brief one-page outline of an operational problem they needed to solve and, similarly, another one-pager for a "people" problem.

For myself, I set the rule that I must pick the biggest and/or most difficult one as the case we would work on. You can imagine my fears when I discovered the worst operational problem among those brought was one that had been in existence for some years and was eating around 10 man-days a month to keep it under control. No-one had managed to find a solution during that time.

My first reaction was to toss it to one side and select an easier "low hanging fruit" case but my conscience bugged me and I finally followed my own rules, using the rationale that at least it would take us through the entire process from beginning to end!

Putting it simply, the process enabled the team of participants to crack the problem with a simple and almost obvious solution, much to the total surprise of all, including myself. The person who brought it with him was literally bouncing in his seat with joy and exclaiming "why didn't we see that ourselves?"

A few months later he reported the problem had been totally eradicated.

After another case or two bringing successful results, I decided to go further by introducing this as a form of consultancy to line managers and their teams with a view to gradually handing over the reins to them as they learnt the concepts.

This would create a tangible contribution to the results in the field. It would also be a distinct difference from the Training function being considered an ivory tower far removed from the harsh reality of problems in the real world of work!

Unfortunately, I ran only two "consultancy" sessions before I was moved to a new job within the bank. However, these two sessions did add even more value for me too because I experienced a couple of "aha!" moments I did not expect.

One was how, when faced with a problem and given an opportunity to work on ideas for solving it together, the activity built an unbelievably strong team spirit that evidenced enthusiastic co-operation towards the vexing problems of colleagues, perhaps for the first time by the manager and the group together.

The second was a very difficult situation where the activity of one team member was apparently causing a lot of problems for the others. They all wanted to lynch the poor guy!

That was the atmosphere that pervaded at the outset.

A centralised function under this manager was causing difficulties to all the other branch managers. At the end of the session devoted to this problem, it so transpired that those with the "complaint" solved it by themselves. They not only suggested what they could do but also implemented the actions necessary to get rid of it. That was quite a turnaround! (This session will be used as an illustration in a short while.)

Why have I gone into the history of this subject? There are two reasons. The first is to show the process I will outline has been used and has been successful with many more cases since those early days. It is not just theory.

The second reason is that this was a pivotal point in my life's work. Having experienced a taster of consultancy, I was very interested in the idea of becoming a management consultant to be able to face many more difficult situations and helping people find a way of solving them. Fortunately, this was to come to fruition some years later and quickly became my passion.

## *What is The Problem Solving Workshop?*

In short, it is a method of introducing managers to a practical approach to problem solving. The concept combines the skills, knowledge, expertise and ideas of people with techniques and disciplines to provide a powerful means of creating new solutions and opportunities.

## *How we get the ball rolling.*

Rather than just spell out what to do and how, I will relate the basic process as if it is a live situation. In fact, it is very much based on the case I briefly mentioned earlier as it does include certain other vital factors to highlight some of the very important considerations that need to be made when undertaking such a programme. One example is the attitude of the manager, as you will see.

> "Even though I took over the area some time ago," Sumit admitted. "It seems that I just cannot make any progress with my team."
>
> I looked at him questioningly, without comment.
>
> "I can't get everyone moving forward as a cohesive unit," he elaborated. "I suppose it's because they are spread across several offices throughout the city."
>
> "Have you tried meetings, Sumit?" I asked.

He laughed derisively. "Oh yes! But you know what these things are like. Nothing much ever gets achieved and everyone feels it is a waste of valuable time when there are so many pressing problems to be sorted out back at their offices."

"Problems?"

"Yes, Nigel. They do get a lot of operational problems, one way and another and, on top of that, there is the constant pressure to get results. We are always all hands to the pumps to keep the boat from sinking and there just isn't the time to think in terms of manning oars or setting a course.

"Knowing this, I must admit that I feel very awkward calling them for the monthly meetings, let alone throwing at them yet another call for additional statistics or reports that Head Office always seem to want ..."

"Yesterday, by any chance?"

"If not sooner."

"Summing up then, there are operating problems to get rid of and a need to build a cohesive, goal-oriented team that is achieving challenging targets."

"If only it were as easy as you make it sound, Nigel," he said bluntly. "Quite frankly, we seem to be staring an impossibility in the face. That sounds closer to the reality of it."

"I was summing up the situation, Sumit. Not proposing that as a solution," I carefully pointed out.

"Sorry, Nigel. I suppose I am a little sensitive to the situation after a few months of facing it day in and day out."

"I don't envy you Sumit, I assure you. However, let's see what can be done to make things easier at least. Would you be prepared to accept the possibility that you and your team could perhaps be so involved in a situation where you may not be able to see the wood for the trees?"

"I would be wrong to disagree with that," he replied truthfully. This seemed to arouse his interest. "Perhaps, as an outsider, you could bring in a different viewpoint which we had overlooked in the rush and tear of pumping water. What can be done to help my team?"

"You'll hate me for this," I promised, smiling wryly. "But I do suggest a meeting ... Now don't look at me like that! This will be a meeting aimed at discussing and solving some of the more pressing problems the team members face."

"We've tried it and it doesn't work," Sumit assured me vehemently. "That sort of meeting degenerates into accusations and arguments and dissolves into an uncontrollable riot. It quickly destroys whatever team spirit that might have existed before the meeting began. I've learnt that the hard way."

"Supposing we try something a little different? This is a slightly unusual approach and, as you have said, they really do need help."

"It sounds good,' Sumit conceded. 'But what guarantee of success can you offer?"

"Absolutely none. There never can be with ventures of this nature. However, my experience is such that I have built up a great deal of confidence in this method of working. The most critical element for success is really in your hands rather than mine, though."

He was a little taken aback by this remark. "What is that?" he asked.

"Sometimes, the problem is caused by the boss or the boss's office! My own subsequent observations have tended to support this viewpoint, too."

"Nigel, I don't put obstacles in the way of my team. I'd be mad if I did. I want them to perform well, so why should I try to stop them?"

"I don't doubt that for one minute but let's look at this from a slightly different angle. Could it be possible that there are things that you are doing — or not doing — that might be causing problems, directly or indirectly, even though you may not be aware of it?"

"I shouldn't think so. If I was causing problems, my team would be darned quick to tell me about it, rather like the way they make themselves painfully clear about meetings being such a waste of time."

"Do you make sure you tell your boss about all the things that she does wrong or which cause you problems?"

"I value my job ... Oh! I see what you mean. Maybe my team could be wary of telling the truth?"

"Yes. On top of that, we sometimes don't realise that a certain action is causing the problem until we really do find time to sit down and analyse the situation properly."

"I will be happy to change whatever is needed if it is possible and if it is going to help the team to achieve more," he confirmed confidently.

"That's good but when such things hit us, we naturally tend to respond less positively than when we sit quietly and rationalise about it. We usually react negatively when we are faced with what seems to be a criticism of ourselves or something we have done. We naturally rise to our own defence rather than discuss the issue coolly and rationally. It is often a difficult reaction for anyone to control."

Sumit was silent for a moment or two as he thought this through for a few minutes, relating these statements to some of his own experiences. "Yes," he finally said. "I see what you mean. So if someone appears to be attacking me, I will need to tread very carefully, keep calm and listen?"

"Exactly," I confirmed. "Sumit, you now seem well in tune with what is needed to make this Problem Solving Workshop more likely to succeed," I advised him.

"We must now plan the preparatory work," I continued. "It's quite simple. We only have to request each of your managers to keep a small notepad in his pocket or briefcase or close at hand at all times and use this to build a list on a daily basis. What we need them to list is all the problems they face."

"They could do that from the top of their heads at any time," he pointed out. "They are quick enough to do this whenever I throw a demand for stats or a report their way."

"True. To begin with, they will list the things which are more obvious. However, by keeping the notepad nearby, they will hopefully jot down less obvious things which may nevertheless be important. Basically, we are far less likely to miss anything of value by doing it this way."

Sumit agreed he would communicate all this to the team.

"Only one thing left now," I announced with a smile. "Find yourself a nice big notepad."

"Naturally," he agreed. "I am bound to have more problems than all of them put together."

"No, but you will do."

"Why do you always talk in riddles?"

"Sumit, I promise you that once the team open up, you will find that there will be a fair number of things for which you will be responsible in order to make their targets achievable. You have to do three things which will determine how successful the whole project is."

"Why is so much dependent upon me? It all seems a bit unfair!"

"Very simple. You managers are paid to have problems! Seriously, apart from noting what they are going to do, you will need to:

- Make careful notes of the actions which you need to undertake and the dates by which they need to be completed.

- Make sure you do undertake them.

- Keep the team informed of progress in respect of each of these points."

"I keep them informed of my progress?" He was astounded. "Who is supposed to be in charge and who is reporting to whom?" He asked a little bluntly. He then added, just for good measure: "won't they all have enough of their own action plans to worry about without having to be concerned about my progress?"

"Let's remind ourselves of the objective behind the list you are going to build during he meeting. What are you doing it for?"

"I thought the idea was for me to do things which require my input or authority to enable them to do a better job."

"A question, Sumit. If your boss agreed to do something to help you to achieve better results — especially if it means that she has agreed to change the way she has been doing things in he past, what would your reaction be?"

"I'll believe it when ... You've done it to me again, haven't you!"

"It's merely the usual approach of putting yourself in the other person's shoes and seeing how much they pinch!" I replied with a grin. "Anyway, I think we have covered enough points for one day. Shall we fix the date for the Problem Solving Workshop and clarify how you will find it most comfortable to sell the idea down the line?"

## At the Workshop.

"First of all," Sumit said to his assembled team of managers. "Thank you for sparing the time to support this new idea. It is something that I trust is going to help us all to get some nasty problems out of the way so that we can improve our productivity. I think you will all agree that it would be rather nice if we could accomplish a lot more with a minimum degree of additional effort."

It brought a few wry chuckles but the group did seem to accept the fact that he was trying to find ways of helping them.

He then introduced me.

"Nigel has heard how difficult things have been and he has arranged today to help us try to find some solutions," he announced. He then handed the meeting over to me.

"Many thanks, Sumit. First of all, gentlemen, I would like to state that my role here today is merely that of a catalyst. I will provide the lead through a process but the actual content and decision making will be entirely down to yourselves and Sumit.

"What we are going to do is to identify some key problems and then pool our ideas for tackling them. We are well away from the distractions of the office environment so that we may use the relative calm of this room to allow us to think more clearly.

"I believe Sumit has asked you all to compile a list of the sort of troubles you face. To get the maximum out of the day, we are going to need to prioritise. The method I suggest is that you go through your list and mark the three most serious problems. By 'serious' I mean one which, if solved, would have the greatest impact on the results of the area for which you are responsible."

I then issued three small index cards to each person and asked them to write their three most serious problems on the cards, one to a card.

Once completed, I had them sit in three groups of four.

"Although each of you faces certain problems," I said. "We need to think more widely for the best results. We may find that more than one office is facing the same problem and solving this particular issue may serve to assist more than one of you. We will therefore make a bigger contribution to you as a team than by solving an issue which relates to one office only.

"Please would each group now compare cards and see if any problems are duplicated. If so, keep only one of the cards, mark it with the total number of cards which related to that problem and discard the duplicates.

"When that is over, I would like the group to sort the cards into priority order: this time it is based on which problem, if solved, would have the biggest impact on the region. To save time, please stop once you have identified the first three. We will then compare notes before proceeding further."

A hubbub of activity ensued. This lasted about ten minutes and then I approached the first flip chart.

"Now we need to prioritise for the region," I announced. "I will ask each group in turn to read out their number one problem and I will write it onto the chart."

This I proceeded to do and there was complete accordance throughout the team: they had all pinpointed the same problem as the most troublesome. It was to do with stationery deliveries from the centralised unit.

The second most important list contained two which were similar. The third level brought another three different items into play.

"Sumit," I said, throwing the ball into his court. "Looking at this from your broader level, are you happy with the priorities which the group has determined or are there any changes which should be made?"

Sumit did agree with the group's findings publicly, although afterwards, he admitted he was privately a little uncertain that the stationery was causing that much trouble. Yes, he had heard grumblings now and again, but that is only to be expected.

I then asked the group to state what the actual problem was on the stationery front and, from there, why it was considered such an important issue compared with the other points raised.

The problem was given as:

> short, late and/or non-delivery of the orders.

The major reasons for it being considered so important were:

- shortages of specialised, particularly sequentially numbered security forms, meant that customer service and internal processing work were being severely affected.

- Keeping a note of what was not received and then following it up and/or reordering the shortfall was taking up time.

- Telephoning around to other offices to obtain a loan of stationery which was vital, getting delivery of it, recording and monitoring the "paying back" was also creating unnecessary work.

I noted these points onto a second flip chart as they were thrown forward by various members of the group. I then asked where the stationery came from. It was explained that one of the offices had a very large storage area and this was therefore utilised to create a centralised control for stationery ordering and delivery in order to gain the benefits of bulk purchasing.

"Is the manager of that branch responsible for the centralised stationery unit?" I asked.

In response, Dhruv confirmed this and that he was the manager concerned.

I asked Dhruv to come to the open end of the horseshoe seating arrangement and to sit facing the rest of the group. "You are probably feeling a bit vulnerable sitting there," I quipped cheerfully to keep things low key. "In fact, I am placing you in a hot seat for a very good reason."

Turning to the group, I told them "Dhruv is facing problems in trying to provide an effective service to the offices. What we must therefore do now is to ask him to tell us what he sees as the circumstances which are preventing him from doing his job the way he would like to."

I then stepped out of the centre stage to the flip chart.

Looking a little nervous, Dhruv commenced the task. "Actually, there are three primary reasons which contribute to this," he said.

"One is that we sometimes get the orders from offices too late to process them in time for the deliveries. The ..."

"That's not right!" Milind suddenly yelled out, rising from his chair in his intensity. I noticed strong nods from the rest of the group who appeared in total accord with him. "Even when the orders are submitted well in time, we still don't get the delivery and ..."

"Sorry to interrupt you," I quickly interjected loudly and a little forcibly but, nevertheless, politely as I strode purposefully to stand between the accuser and the accused to break the eye contact. "Dhruv did mention that there were three reasons and we have only given him the opportunity to mention one of them. Could the issue you have in mind be one of the other two he wishes to list?"

Milind looked a little startled. He then frowned as he realised what he was doing. "I am sorry," he said sheepishly. As I walked back to the flip chart, he again apologised, this time directly to Dhruv and then sat down.

Sumit was also somewhat taken aback by this outburst. This subject was even more fraught with emotion than he had expected. It really was beginning to dawn on him that the concerns about stationery were far more deep-rooted than he had realised until now.

Dhruv continued. "The second reason is that orders exceed the planned stock drawings by offices by such a large extent that even the reserves are totally exhausted most of the time for a number of items. As a result, we are unable to supply or the stock levels then dictate a quota system to ensure all get at least something with which to work"

"Yes," Milind interjected in total agreement. "That's the issue I was steaming about just now. That's the one which hurts us a good deal. I shouldn't have jumped down your throat like that, Dhruv, it was totally uncalled for."

Dhruv shrugged. "Don't worry, Milind. No offence taken. I know it causes a lot of trouble," he said with sincerity.

He then went on. "The final issue is the problem of transport. We do not get the use of the company van when we need it, in spite of the planned usage agreed by and with Head Office. They keep pulling rank on us, so to speak, and we end up being told that it is out on some urgent mission or other and we will have to wait until it is next free."

Meanwhile, I paraphrased these three issues onto the flip chart as Dhruv listed them. "Is any one of these causing much more trouble than either of the others?"

"The lack of available transport is by far the worst of all. It causes no end of trouble."

"Followed by?"

"Ordering being greater than the offices' original plans."

I numbered them in that order. 'To get the greatest improvement for the area, then, we must concentrate upon the transport problem first. Then we can move on to the other two in sequence.

"I would now like to outline the process I suggest we put into practice for tackling this ..."

"But surely this is something completely outside our jurisdiction," interrupted Pawan suddenly. "I know for a fact that Dhruv has complained on a number of occasions to Head Office, even to fairly senior managers, but to no avail. I have also taken this up separately to help bolster his argument, but either they don't care or are in no position to do anything about it. Either way, nothing happens and we have to continue facing the same old problems."

There was a chorus of support from the rest of the group.

"Surely they should get another van," suggested another member of the team helpfully.

"That has been suggested to them but they say the cost does not ..."

"Gentlemen, please!" I interjected, raising my voice above the growing noise level.

On gaining their attention, I then continued on a calmer note. "The process I would like us to follow is to avoid trying to find solutions until we have studied this situation in greater depth."

"I'm sorry if I sound critical or negative," Pawan said openly. "But it does appear that we cannot really go any deeper. It is pretty cut and dried. It is out of our power to do anything about it and surely it is a problem that we are just going to have to continue to live with."

"I agree that it does seem to be a bit of a lost cause," I replied matter-of-factly. "However, I would like to look at this from a slightly different viewpoint, which is: what we are going through today is really a pilot project. A learning exercise. We need to experiment with, and thereby understand more fully, a different way of approaching problems.

"The benefit of tackling an unsolvable problem first is that it gives us a good opportunity to work through the process from beginning to end. This will enable us to consider the approach and make adjustments to make it more effective for the future.

"On this basis, can we put this one down to useful experience?"

I turned to Sumit. 'What do you say, Sumit?'

He suggested that the managers should decide for themselves what they thought might be best.

The group then discussed it through very briefly and they all finally agreed with the idea.

My next task was to summarise the process so far:

- List problems over a period of time to ensure as many problems as possible are brought into the open.

- There should be particular emphasis on: "situations, perhaps recurrent, which use a lot of your time." This should help bring out areas which are considered "unsolvable" and which are no longer regarded as problems but more as a part of life.

- Prioritise the list on the basis of: which problem, on being solved, would bring the greatest results to the area for which you are responsible? This maximises the benefits to be gained.

- In the case of a number of units/departments joining together on such a Problem Solving Workshop, the problems have to be prioritised in a similar way but, this time, based on what will bring the greatest benefits to the overall area the participants represent between them.

- Select the problem with the greatest potential to be analysed in the Workshop.

This done, I then continued: "We have identified the problems that Dhruv faces and also managed to prioritise these. Now, before we look for answers to the problem, we must make sure we understand the question properly! "At this stage, we must put Dhruv back in the 'hot seat' and question him in some depth about the problem with the van. All of us must try to understand the problem fully. We have to ensure that we are not working from preconceived biases instead of the facts.

"In other words we do not want to try to apply a cure for the wrong illness!

"My experience has shown that, in a group of this size, we are likely to find more than one way of viewing a situation. One or two people may approach the subject from totally different standpoints, which could lead the group thinking differently towards an effective solution.

"There is one more very important issue which I have to stress. During this phase, we do not attempt to find solutions! We only seek to clarify all aspects of the situation, no more than that. Any attempts to put forward solutions will be squashed!"

To emphasise this point, I wrote boldly on a fresh sheet of chart paper:

"NO SOLUTIONS ACCEPTED!"

After checking that everyone understood and accepted the concept, I said "I'll start the ball rolling if I may. Dhruv, according to your plan, how many hours a week do you require to take the van?"

The questioning went on from there. Yes, there were a few premature attempts to offer a solution and, when this did occur, members of the team jovially shouted the solution monger down.

It was a good twenty minutes or more before the questioning finally died down. I think we all learnt something new about the problem.

Another interesting factor which struck me was in the reactions I observed in the team. One noticeable example occurred fairly early on in the proceedings.

There was a question which had sounded a little pointed and almost accusing towards Dhruv and his performance. I very tactfully intervened and suggested that our mission was to try to understand the situation in order to attempt to find a solution to it rather than to cast aspersions at anyone. This was very readily accepted and adopted by the managers. From then on, words were noticeably far more carefully chosen and more sensitively delivered.

I also noticed that, as a result of that positive change in his colleagues, Dhruv appeared to become more open with the facts. It was almost as if an invisible wall of defensiveness had been removed.

With the questions over, I came back onto the scene. "Do we all understand the situation now?" I asked.

There were very worried frowns accompanying the silent nods.

"Then let's write down the major aspects of the problem as we see it."

Javed was the first to voice the feelings of the group. "It really does seem to be the way that Pawan described it earlier on, I'm afraid," he ventured. "We have a situation here where poor Dhruv is well and truly stuck between a rock and a hard place. There appears to be no avenue, not within our control, anyway, that can be pursued to get the van more regularly, or any other vehicle for that matter, to enable him to get the deliveries out at the frequency needed to satisfy our requirements."

"Can we put that another way, preferably in a shorter form, for me to write it on the chart?"

"Mission impossible?" quipped a joker in the pack. It was a much-needed morale booster. We needed something to laugh about to lighten the gloom of the meeting for a while.

"Can we put the problem in the form of an objective?"

"How to obtain transport for more time each week?" Suggested another individual.

I wrote this up. "Any other ways of looking at it?"

Pawan gave a wry chuckle. "How do you make sure that you don't need the transport for as much time each week! That seems easier to me!"

This brought a roar of cynical laughter.

I wrote the comment up on the chart, much to everyone's surprise.

"Hey, what are you doing?" interjected Pawan suddenly sitting forward in his chair in a more serious vein. By contrast, his colleagues laughed all the more because of my action and Pawan's obvious discomfort. "Why did you write that up? I was only joking!"

"As I mentioned earlier, when looking at a problem, there can be more than one viewpoint. Even though it may have been in jest, it could nonetheless raise some thoughts later on, so why discard it?"

Pawan merely shrugged his shoulders and sat back to signal his defeat, much to the further amusement of the others.

No further suggestions were forthcoming, so I had to move on to the next step. "We have two objectives stated here,' I said, pointing to the flip chart. If we can find ways of achieving either or, better still both, then we might be better off than we are now.

"The next phase in this process is to start generating alternative ideas for solutions. One of the best ways of doing this is a brainstorming session.

"Let me explain how this works. Everyone throws forward ideas as they come into their heads and I will write them onto a flip chart. However, there are some rules that must be strictly observed. One of these is that even if the idea seems silly, don't hold it back, give it! This promotes creative thinking and expands the potential for getting something that might work.

It therefore follows that if we hear an idea which sounds silly, or even unworkable, we do not comment upon it or criticise it in any way. It is more constructive to think of a better idea."

I then had them thinking around the topic of how to obtain some form of transport more often. Yes a few funny ideas did come up and were recorded accordingly and they did seem to bring a different or unusual slant to the picture. However, in spite of all this, there did seem to be a general air of defeat after a very short space of time.

Much to Pawan's disgust, I then pointed towards the second objective of how to ensure that transport was not needed so much and turned to a fresh page on the flip chart to start logging the ideas.

"Fewer deliveries?" questioned Gautam.

I scribbled that up hastily.

Gautam shook his head in disbelief. "But that was a question, we can't live with fewer ..."

"No criticisms," I interrupted incisively. "Not even of your own ideas!"

"But that would mean larger deliveries," cut in Milind in defence of Gautam.

So I wrote 'larger deliveries' under the previous statement.

"How can we take larger deliveries unless we have storage space at ...?"

The presenter of that criticism was cut off in mid argument by a colleague but meanwhile I added 'more storage at offices' to the list.

"That's a point," interjected Javed suddenly. "Over the past month or two I have been doing some reorganising and clearing out in the office and as a result have quite a bit of redundant storage space. Would it help if I took a monthly delivery instead of the usual weekly one?"

I was about to interrupt but then thought it better to let this conversation flow, even if it was away from the stated objective of generating alternative solutions.

Dhruv's eyes had lit up. "That would save me three journeys a month" he responded.

"If that would help, I could do the same," offered Pawan.

That set the ball rolling. The team started putting their heads together and two or three offers of taking fortnightly deliveries came up from managers who had less available space. They then moved on to work out how they could plan the deliveries within the constraints that Dhruv had been facing.

In their excitement to button up the scheme, Sumit and I were totally ignored. I looked at Sumit and smiled, indicating that we should leave them to it for a while and see what transpires.

It was a fascinating scene, watching the managers working busily together as a team, all intent on making the idea work. What struck me more than anything else was the total change in the direction of the group. Originally, the subject had been such a highly emotive one with a lot of discontent being aimed at Dhruv, with strong expectations from the group that he would have to improve things. Now the situation had defused to the extent that the problem was being solved by the complainants changing what they were doing in order to sort the situation out.

It wasn't too long before there was a unanimous cheer. "We've done it!" came the triumphant chorus from several mouths.

I took the opportunity to break up the huddle and get the meeting back into some semblance of order. "Can we just go through the formality of charting the conclusions you have come to, please?" I asked, holding out the marker pen to Javed, who had been leading the discussions and held the pad with the conclusions on it.

Javed came forward and charted the newly agreed frequency of deliveries for each office, then added the delivery schedule that the team had arrived at to satisfy this.

"Dhruv, Does this look feasible to you, bearing in mind the current availability of transport?"

Dhruv happily nodded his assent.

"Is everyone else happy with this first cut?" I asked and received an affirmative answer.

I then turned to Sumit. "This is a change in the schedule of deliveries and to an extent goes against the centralisation policy which had been laid down some two years or so ago, isn't it?"

He agreed.

"Then whose approval should this have?"

"Strictly speaking, my boss's," he replied. "However, it is a minor adjustment in view of the fact that the policy did away with semi-annual ordering by all offices directly with suppliers to obtain cost savings. Quite frankly, this is a change which is vital. I would prefer that we try out this scheme you have all devised and if it proves successful, which I am sure it will, I will then advise my boss that it has been done and how it is working."

This statement brought approving nods from the managers.

"So it has your approval for implementation?"

"Without doubt," replied Sumit. "All I would like to add is that I feel that everyone has done an excellent job in solving this terrible problem. Well done, everyone."

There were satisfied smiles. However, there was a sudden interruption.

"But this is really incredible when you think about it," Dhruv said excitedly. Everyone looked at him enquiringly. "Well, this seemed to be such an impossible thing to solve and, as others said, totally outside our area of control. Yet we have actually found an answer within those seemingly impossible constraints!

"Not only that, the answer was really so simple that we must have been daft not to have seen it before."

There were noises of agreement.

"It is a combination of things," I pointed out. "First, there is the magical power of teamwork. The synergetic effect of people working closely together with open minds. Then there is the fact that we are cocooned from the outside world. We are away from the daily routine, the rush and tear to get things done. We can step back and analyse the situation more carefully. We begin to see the wood instead of being buried in the branches and twigs of the trees."

## A brief summary of the disciplines.

- The person facing the problem is placed in the "hot seat" and is questioned about the facts of the situation.

- No attempts to provide a solution must be allowed, the objective is to make sure the problem is fully understood.

- This stage also enables different viewpoints to emerge, to give wider scope for the generation of alternative solutions later.

- Another important point here is that the cause of the problem should be investigated thoroughly.

- In doing this, the question "why?" is vital. It should keep being applied to the answer given until we can probe no further. This also helps to ensure that we finally focus upon the real cause and try to cure that rather than a symptom. This is such an important part of the process that it is discussed in more depth a little later in this chapter.

- The problem should then be defined in terms of objectives. Again, different viewpoints are constructive. Even stating the same objectives in different ways can positively affect the quest for a good solution.

- Brainstorm to generate as many alternative solutions as possible for each of the stated objectives.

- Analyse each alternative (or combination of alternatives) to determine which will best satisfy the objectives.

The facilitation by an outsider helps remove "hierarchical" barriers to some extent but it is nevertheless essential that the manager, as the head of the team, must be present because the authority to decide will often rest with him/her. The team is unable to make some decisions and, if the manager is not present and did not hear the reasoning behind the proposal, s/he may reject it without understanding the full implications. This would potentially result in lower morale and engagement — as well as lost opportunity.

The illustration also shows how the team were facilitated in terms of process and disciplines, helped with the thinking process. The content was entirely theirs. This is an important factor to understand because the question arising from the event is: why can't the manager undertake the process with the team? If the manager does this on a regular basis, as and when needed, the need for an external facilitator (expense!) is removed and we can just get on with it rather than waiting for a consultant's availability.

This is a view I genuinely support. It was in fact part of the thinking in the initial stages of building the Problem Solving Workshop concept: helping managers learn to do this for themselves. The biggest stumbling block, however, is the manager. It is not easy to let go and apparently "lose control." There are natural fears: will the team decide on something that won't work? Will they really have the interests of the company at heart? Will they understand enough about the circumstances to be able to come to the right conclusions? And so on.

Yet, if you consider this live example, the entire team was pushing to find a solution to their problem. They were determined to get an outcome. They had the interests of the organisation in mind. They did not know all the circumstances but the process enabled them to learn what they were.

This particular episode was not the only one where these kinds of behaviours were evident. I have witnessed it time and again. My experience has been that there is often an unexpected solution rather like the one in this case. On top of this, there is a sense of achievement within the team and a total, and I mean total, commitment to making the solution work.

If we want to be Pioneering Powerful Performance, we need to learn to trust people and their abilities. We have to facilitate the thinking process and the disciplines it entails. We do not do all the thinking. We do not come up with all the solutions.

Our role is to help the team succeed. Full stop!

In order to do this, there are a couple of extremely vital concepts to practice that are described in more detail in this book:

- "Leading from Behind"
- "Ask! Don't Tell!"

Once you have mastered these, you will be able to undertake more easily and effectively the facilitation of powerful Problem Solving Workshops.

## The importance of "Why"

As was briefly mentioned earlier, the question "Why?" is crucial to getting to the real cause of the problem. All too often, we chase into finding a cause, then apply a solution based on this without checking whether what we have identified is the root of the issue or not. We then wonder why the time and effort invested in the activity brings little or no results.

It is necessary to treat the underlying cause(s), not the visible symptoms.

Unfortunately, I see the "curing the symptoms" happening as a regular feature in quite a number of cases.

## The "rule of thumb" regarding the question "Why?"

Quite simply, to keep asking "Why" until it can no longer be answered! However, beware of the possibility that it may not be answerable because of lack of knowledge and may therefore mean we need to go and investigate more before commencing the search for alternative solutions.

## 2.5. Enhancing the Action Planning.

*SYNOPSIS:*

*Enhancing the impact — getting our direct reports to use these tools and techniques to achieve more with their teams — cascading downward.*

-=.=.=.-

Although there is little to add beyond what was covered in Part 1 about building the Action Plans themselves, there is more to consider that can add further value and power to the process in general.

We have seen (and if you have tried what was outlined in Part 1, you will have experienced) how this process creates so much positivity for undertaking appraisals because achievements have been documented. Therefore, if there are people who report to our direct reports, we can help these managers cascade the concept downward to them.

The KRA meeting guidance notes will be slightly different because we will potentially looking across all KRAs and may involve the individual tackling several KRA Action Plans concurrently.

As our direct reports get comfortable with the process, including the "Ask! Don't tell!" approach, we can coach them to work in a similar way. In fact, the probability is that the few forward thinkers among them will seek to do this fairly early because of the positive experience they have had with it and also want their people to experience this.

A live example of this was illustrated at the latter end of the case study given at the end of Chapter 2.1. Getting More Than A Vision.

If we can help our direct reports succeed in this way, the overall results of our area are likely to increase significantly, and along with it the levels of morale, job satisfaction and staff retention. It is that powerful.

## 2.6. Controls: Enhancing our monitoring system.

*SYNOPSIS:*

*Using monitoring checks to ensure achievements do not slide backwards again while we are not looking. Also a word of caution regarding unwitting complacency.*

.=.=.=.

We had covered all but this KRA before talking of Action Planning. There was a reason for this: Controls include the monitoring of Action Plans, so it seemed logical to place it here rather than earlier with the other KRA items.

We saw in Chapter 1.6. there are three kinds of monitoring necessary to check we are on course.

   i. Ensuring the action steps are rolling out as planned.

   ii. Ensuring the expected results are happening.

   iii. Ensuring the results are maintained.

Now that we are deeper into the concepts and processes, we should take a closer look at the last item.

### *iii. Ensuring the results are maintained.*

As a part of the six KRA area of Controls, devising simple but effective self-audit methods for monitoring our standards on a regular basis provides us an early warning system. Here too, the criticality of the subject matter will determine the periodicity of the self-audit and perhaps the depth of it.

For these activities, formats will need to be designed to make the checks consistent and self-explanatory. A "reminder" diary system for them will also be important to ensure none are overlooked.

Let's take a look at some suggested aspects that can be measured. You will need to consider what else might be of important in your area of responsibility and devise ways of monitoring them.

- Health & Safety. Example: a "walk-about" to check specific requirements such as no trailing electrical wires, emergency exits are not blocked nor their doors unopenable, first-aid boxes are properly stocked. These would be relatively regular checks, such as monthly or potentially more frequently, whereas a check of the due date for fire extinguisher servicing might be half-yearly.

- Standards from all KRAs: Checks to ensure we are not exceeding Budgets (nor likely to); Quality is being maintained in the various aspects of what we provide; Sales are normally monitored quite closely as a matter of course. The same follows for timeliness but the more difficult one is Staff Morale, of course, but there will be some regular checks that will no doubt help.

*Let's take a look at some points relating to the standards of all KRAs.*

As mentioned in Chapter 2.3.5. On Timeliness, we might decide that we need to improve our performance for a particular process. We build a plan, execute it and it works. We have brought the processing time down to 5 minutes, as planned. Now, how critical is this standard? If it is a priority, then we can log performance on a daily basis to enable a regular (monthly?) review to ensure it is not slipping.

We must consider what information or data needs to be logged and how we should do so. We may later find, particularly as we start analysing, that we need to improve it by adding useful and relevant information but on the other hand we must avoid the temptation to add too much else the task of collecting it will possibly outweigh the potential benefits of the exercise!

In doing this, we need to think carefully about the implications of what is being measured and also how the audit data are to be analysed. Being happy that the findings show we are within the targeted levels may prevent us from spotting the potential "hidden" problem lurking behind the numbers. Let me repeat the specific example from earlier that explains this clearly.

When in a client company, I reviewed the performance measurements for errors in the typing pool. These revealed a very low margin of error of which they were justly proud. Their rate was 2% against the 5% maximum error standard set.

My analysis showed that 7-10 rejections out of the 15-20 that happened each day were in one kind of letter only. It was an awkward letter because it was lengthy, full of detail, tabulated and had to be formatted every time.

On investigation, it was found that the major problem was the formatting. All other letters were pre-formatted as templates by the Supervisor and thus only required input of the variable information. This particular set of letters had not been formatted as templates and all the concentration on the intricate formatting caused errors in other input.

Realising the time, cost, and frustration that this was causing, the Supervisor immediately agreed to format the letter that day to standardise it. These specific frustrations and errors were soon a thing of the past and, as a further benefit, their quality standard was even better than before.


This live case study shows how even high standards can potentially be improved and "hidden" problems brought out onto the table for solving if you are willing to analyse what is happening rather than just accept that things are going well.

# 2.7. Reporting.

*SYNOPSIS:*

*Some key issues to consider when formalising a process for team members to report to us and for us to consolidate and report upwards, thus ensuring effective communication.*

*This is very important for another crucial reason — it consolidates the achievements of our team members as well as for ourselves, creating the foundations for positive and accurate appraisal contents.*

-=-=-=-

A simple and concise way of reporting progress is of great importance in more than one way.

- We need to be updated on progress across our area of responsibility, necessitating useful feedback coming from our direct reports.

- We must also keep our boss informed so that s/he is kept fully aware of what is happening/not happening.

## *Reports from our direct reports.*

For the most part, this will be updates on the activities involved in the current Action Plans, plus the monthly reporting from the Control checks. On top of this, what plans are to be started in the coming calendar month. We will no doubt need to undertake a brief review session with each of them to deal with any clarifications that may be needed.

The specimen Action Plan Summary format in Section 1.6. "Building a Monitoring System" (Figure 2) can help make the process more simple and straightforward. The reports will be easier to assimilate if they are divided into the KRAs and this also helps with the summarising of them.

If an Action Plan has been completed during the month, then the results of the plan should be measured and reported. This is necessary to be able to define what has been achieved, which may be as per expectations or more than/less than expectations. If the result is significantly lower than planned, perhaps another approach is needed should the original target be a vitally important one.

There is also another very important aspect to this. These reports will be the foundation of the Appraisal Review at year-end. These are the documented proofs of their performance and ensure nothing is overlooked.

Plans for their individual growth should also be included (see Chapter 2.3.4. Staff Morale) to ensure progress is monitored on these plans as well as to make sure people do not feel their needs are being forgotten.

## Reporting upwards to our manager.

We will need to summarise the inputs from the team and ourselves in order to keep the report short, concise and helpful. Again, it is advisable to summarise by KRA.

Dependent upon their number, we can perhaps summarise the Action Plans in four categories with the targets given in brief:

- Completed (with brief mention of actual results).

- On schedule.

- Behind schedule (with brief information on what is being done about the situation).

- New plans due to commence in the next calendar month (with brief outline of the results aimed for).

We should also enumerate the Control checks undertaken and their results, which can be simply laid out in a spread sheet with a column for "In Order". A separate column will show any irregularities, with a further column to outline what has been/is being done to rectify the shortfall and, if necessary, what is being done to prevent it happening again.

By keeping our boss informed in this way, it enables him/her to question items and also to re-prioritise our plans if needed.

One last, fairly important point I should raise here is that these reports to our boss will also provide the backbone of our own performance appraisal!

## 2.8. Performance Management and the use of Appraisals.

*SYNOPSIS:*

*Using the recorded results in creating strong and very positive appraisal experiences.*

-=-=-=-

A part of our role as a manager is to conduct Appraisals. This activity must be a positive experience that sustains morale and performance rather than killing it.

Let's look at some of the ways that Appraisals are transformed into negative experiences for all involved. This will help us better understand the hows and whys of transforming the process into something that is motivational.

## 2.8.1. The Pitfalls of Appraisals.

*SYNOPSIS:*

*The appraisal process is too often regarded negatively by both parties. We briefly examine some of the major causes.*

-=-=-=-

Apart from communications, one of the biggest negatives in staff surveys is the topic of Appraisals. This is understandable because there is so much that can go wrong and, unfortunately, often does. As a result, neither the appraiser nor the appraised really want to undertake the process.

The symptoms are many. For example, what percentage of forms does not reach HR by the deadline? How many reminders have to be issued?

What happens to the forms after the results have been used to set new pay levels, analyse training needs and consider promotions/moves?

As part of the process, KRAs may be set for the coming year and listed in the appraisal form that will be used in the next round. Generally these are stored in HR. Are copies kept by the appraisee and appraiser for them to use during the year or do the KRAs only see the light of day when appraisals are next undertaken?

How much time and effort is put into training both appraiser and the appraised? Is this undertaken every year? What is the cost of this in terms of time, money and in opportunity cost?

Does the process and the format provide quantitative information regarding the outcomes of any training and development measures undertaken to assist an individual's success?

How does the process reduce the problem of differences of evaluation by "hard" vs. "soft" managers?

Does the appraisal format really cover business considerations and also the vital behavioural traits that determine success?

When people are transferred from one role to another, what are processes in place for objectively handling the "split" appraisal? Also, how is the handover of KRAs to the new incumbent managed?

## The Judgement Factor.

One of the biggest contributions to the negative feelings of appraisals can be summed up in one word: "judgement".

People do not like being judged. Managers don't like judging their people. Appraisals are viewed as a rather painful experience and we would rather not do it. This is one of the major contributions to late deliveries.

My view is to take the easy way out. Don't judge people!

Simple!

## But aren't appraisals all about judgement?

Yes.

But we don't have to judge. We can get the individuals to judge themselves.

Some companies will respond to this by saying they get their staff to rate themselves. Great. But what happens next? If their boss responds with "what makes you think you can give yourself this high a rating?" it is rather distant from the ideal.

I am not suggesting all managers in all those companies will respond this way but it is a danger about which we need to be acutely aware.

Another observation is that, generally speaking, people actually underrate their performance. There are exceptions that are the opposite of course.

There is also the temptation — comparing the individual's performance with that of others. Certainly a temptation for ourselves as well as for the person self-appraising. Unfortunately, this approach can be quite negative in its consequences.

Let's be honest. Some people are better at certain things than others — for whatever reasons. Comparing our own performance at running a 100 metre sprint with the performance of Usain Bolt, the Jamaican world-champion sprinter, will wear down our morale.

But this is what tends to happen in the world of work — especially in the sales arena, where performance measurement is pretty much clear and conclusive. How can we make things more positive and motivating?

A more powerful and positive approach is that of comparing ourselves to ourselves. Have I improved upon my previous level of performance and to what extent? As we all like to see we have progressed, knowing we have done so is a very positive boost to our morale.

This approach strongly facilitates the next phase: "what do I want to achieve by this time next year?" Then, from this: "how I want to go about achieving this" will naturally follow.

It is with these points in mind that I advise Sales Managers in particular to adopt this principle when setting the coming year's targets with their direct reports.

## 2.8.2. Making Appraisals Motivational.

*SYNOPSIS:*

*Outlining how the processes we have discussed, together with the new approach to leading, dispel most if not all the negatives that generally occur in the appraisal experience.*

*It goes much further than eradicating negatives. It builds positives in their place.*

-=-=-=-

## *The preparation process.*

If we have followed the activities and processes mentioned in the earlier chapters, most of the preparatory work has already been undertaken.

Because of the regular, positive problem-solving approach with each of our direct reports, especially when shortfalls in performance have been recorded by them and their plans undertaken to straighten these out, the end result is most likely to be a positive appraisal for each and every one of them. This is backed by the evidence, already sent upwards in our own reporting each month, so it cannot be easily refuted.

What helps is the quantification/qualification of the results they have achieved. There is very little that is "woolly" or "fuzzy" about these, thus leaving little room for argument or dissent.

Similarly, when shortfalls in skills or knowledge have been identified as part of the process, these would have generated action plans to assist the individual to "Score Sixes". The result should be that the person will have been able to go on to achieve more effectively and also allowed more to be added to their skills inventory.

These regular interactions with each of our direct reports will also provide an objective picture concerning their abilities. A few examples might be: ability to plan, approach to problem solving, leadership ability and style, communication, attention to detail, realism, etc. This will enable us to rate them accordingly as well as coach them to higher levels.

The initial task is to sort the data and, most likely, the most useful criteria will be initially by KRA and secondly by level of impact upon results under each KRA. This will bring the most significant results to the fore, making it easier to summarise.

With this information available, the individual can quantify and qualify their performance, as can we.

## *Some further considerations.*

It is probably helpful for morale and performance if interim "appraisals" are undertaken, say, every quarter. This process demonstrates that nothing has been forgotten and credit is given where credit is due. It underlines our willingness to be open and fair.

It also allows any previously unspoken issues or performance problems to be brought out and dealt with appropriately (and we definitely must not forget to use "Ask! Don't tell!" when discussing these).

The quarterly review will be of particular importance if we are new to the team we are to manage. The reason I say this is that, if the previous "regime" has been negative, unfair, manipulating (and perhaps more), then we are unlikely to be trusted. This is natural and quite understandable.

The following live case illustrates what has just been stated and how, effectively used, appraisals can help in Pioneering Powerful Performance.

> I took over responsibility for an area comprising around 120 people, having 10-12 management grade staff. The unit had been neglected for years and was in a poor state. There were few management skills, a poor understanding of processes and controls, ineffective organisation and fragmented working. There had been no training to speak of, which did not help one iota.
>
> As a result, quality was not particularly good, costs were high, customer service, although polite, was not particularly fast, and controls were very weak. Staff morale however, was quite good.
>
> The challenge was therefore to bring significant improvements to every aspect of operations — but without destroying staff morale. If anything, it should be enhanced still further.
>
> I had, in another territory with this company, been subject to Management by Objectives (MbO) and the concept of Action Planning had been used in that process. However, it had not been introduced and managed in a particularly positive manner. In fact, it was almost destructive. For example, meeting the target dates was the criteria for judgement rather than meeting the target

itself. Setting target dates was a long and arduous battle, with the boss hammering for too short a time-frame and the reportee jousting for too distant an end date with a final settlement somewhere between the two in compromise.

If all this was not enough, for the correction of weaknesses identified in operations audits were expected to have short-term target dates without any consideration to prioritisation or even the resources available to undertake this work. As a result, all these Action Plans started on the same day: today!

It was a recipe for disaster. It was naturally impossible to meet the end dates and this led to requests for extensions and further battles on target dates. It was acrimonious and led to less than high morale, to put it nicely.

In this branch to which I had freshly arrived, there were no signs of any MbO activities. I therefore wanted to use the Action Planning process but in what I considered to be a more constructive and positive manner.

The planning process started well. I mentioned that we needed to get a rough idea of how long each step of the plan was likely to take so that we could "guesstimate" its ending and therefore the potential start date of the next step. It would also help me to know roughly where I would need to provide support should this be needed and thus plan for myself what resources would be able to be with whom and when.

The words "target date" brought instant negative reactions. Barriers went up. Defence mechanisms were activated.

It appeared that they had also been through similar negative experiences with the company's version of MbO! As much as I argued my differentiators, I was not trusted. This too in spite of the fact that I had not argued about target dates. I had even recommended later target dates where I saw that they could potentially be upset by certain seasonal activity levels or over-optimism. I stressed "guesstimate" and "to give us an idea of when other things might be started" but to no avail.

I did not resent the lack of trust. They did not know me so how could they tell that things would be any different when it came to the real crunch? But it did mean I was stuck. By way of confirmation, I noticed that plans were, generally, not being worked on with the kind of priority that had been discussed.

During the brief checks, I even found some managers had hardly touched the planned work.

Things had to change. I had to find a solution. The only thing I could think of was that they would only trust me if, when the crunch came, I did things the way I claimed I would rather than revert to what they learnt from bitter experience was "MbO Type" behaviour.

I concluded that I would have the first round of interim performance appraisals as 3 months had passed already.

This caused a stir because such reviews were always annual. Once we got started, I made sure I had a couple of people in particular at the front end of the queue. One had completed one of the shorter plans but overshot the target date by a week. When we got to that plan, I said "you planned to eradicate this problem by 26th June and ..."

The manager's immediate response was defensive. "But I finished late because ..."

I looked him in the eye, a little fiercely and interrupted. "I couldn't care less."

His reaction was in his body language. It virtually said "here we go again. I am back to having to fight for justice." This was precisely the reaction I needed.

Before he could say any more, I added "I have only got one question for you."

"What is that?" He enquired, defences obviously on high alert.

"Has the problem gone away?"

"Yes, it has."

"I agree. I have checked and seen it for myself." I then wrote in the comments column of my performance review "Achieved 100%" and I said "Well done. A good step forward."

He looked at me in total surprise. "But I completed it a week late," he almost protested.

"I told you. I couldn't care less. You have hit the target, which was to kill off that problem. You have done it. We only guessed it would take two months, if you remember. Another week is neither here nor there. Shall we move to the next point?"

The change in his attitude was as sudden as it was dramatic. Now he was fired up.

The second individual had not completed a plan and it had virtually come to a standstill. He too became visibly defensive on reaching that item.

"You were going to have the third step in the plan well under way by about now, weren't you?" I asked.

The response was an unhappy, guarded nod.

"But just a moment. I was supposed to give you two extra staff to be able to cope with the first step and I have not been able to thanks to the small project we had thrown at us by the Regional Office. That is not your problem. Its my problem. We are going to have to reschedule this plan once I have the resources again. Shall we move to the next item?"

His face was a picture of surprise. Again, under the old regime, he would have been blasted out of the water for not completing the job as per plan even though vital and promised resources were not supplied.

By bringing things to a head, I was able to demonstrate that I had meant everything I had said. People began to trust me. They started work in earnest and were comfortable seeking my support. They knew that I would go so far as to recognise their work in writing. On top of this, I was particularly delighted that some actually brought out problems that had been kept under the carpet out of fear and we were able to tackle them together.

It was really wonderful to see how the improvements began to take a life of their own and the teams' results were becoming plainly visible. Success seemed to breed success.

The appraisals wrap up a single cycle but, like a wheel, the process keeps rolling to provide continuous improvement, persistently Pioneering Powerful Performance. We may ask ourselves whether we will get to the point where no more improvement can be done. Maybe all that can be done has been done. What then?

The answer is, generally speaking, we live in a world of constant change and perforce we must be alert and untiringly seeking new opportunities to take our performance to higher and higher levels. Competitors come up with new products, the market changes, economic ups and downs have to be coped with. We, however, must be way ahead of the pack.

### 2.8.3. Some other positive benefits.

One major disruption to both the productivity and the appraisal of individuals can occur when someone moves from their role and another person takes over their position.

First, on the work front, the new individual needs to settle in and this may well cause any plans the leaver had started upon being all too easily lost and forgotten in the process.

It is therefore vital that the "formal" handover to the new incumbent includes an introduction and explanation of the plans current and pending. On top of this, there should be an assessment of the current situation in respect of those plans already underway. Then we have a clear, qualified and quantified starting point for the new person, allowing their value addition to be clear at the time of the next quarterly appraisal round.

Secondly, this process will allow our final appraisal to take place immediately for the outgoing party. This ensures their achievements with us will not be overlooked in their annual appraisal should they be moving elsewhere within the organisation.

Finally, it will be important to ensure our new direct report be given the freedom to re-think the plans and, should they feel they want to do things differently, this should be discussed. Any revisions to the actions or priorities can then be made, as appropriate. This can facilitate their ownership of the plans and give them job satisfaction rather than have them feeling constrained by someone else's ideas and approach. They can instead do it their way.

### 2.8.4. Ah! But what about poor performers?

*SYNOPSIS:*

*Accepting the fact there are exceptions and these need to be dealt with in a positive but firm manner — but not without careful considerations on what might be causing the problem as opposed to it being caused by the individual.*

-=-=-=-

In the previous chapter, I blithely stated: "the end result is most likely to be a positive appraisal for each and every one of them." On reading that, I am sure you will have asked the question: "what about poor performers?"

Of course there will be the odd exception. So how do we deal with these unfortunate situations?

If performance has been monitored on a regular basis — perhaps even intensifying these from, say, quarterly to monthly as things were not progressing satisfactorily — we should have some early warning signals upon which both we and the individual should have acted.

Continued lack of progress will have demanded deeper analysis to double-check there were no other external factors that prevented the person from performing (e.g. lack of support from third parties, a process that needs to be changed or the goal was too large or far too complex).

These steps should ascertain we have covered all the options during the course of the period under review: training, guidance, action planning for improvement and the monitoring.

If all these aspects have been carefully taken into account, we can be pretty certain the problem is with our direct report, who will also be painfully aware of their position.

## *But what is the poor performer really like?*

However, there is another important aspect we need to be very much aware of: preferred behaviours. Working extensively with The McQuaig System™ of psychometrics has taught me that our preferred behaviours provide us with certain natural strengths. By the same token, it also means there are behaviours we find more difficult to enact — especially if they form a significant part of our daily routine.

Just to illustrate, some people are patient and steady. They do not rush things and go one step at a time with just one thing at a time, seeing it through to the end before starting another task. They turn tasks into a routine so they run like clockwork.

By way of contrast, we have those who are dynamic and enjoy pressure and deadlines. They are driven and like to multitask with plenty of variety.

Thus, if we expect the patient person to deal with pressure, deadlines and multitasking, they are likely to find it difficult to cope. Similarly, getting the dynamic person to work on steady routine, following a single task through to its end before moving to the next, they will probably get bored.

## *We have to always watch out for clues.*

As we start working with individuals, we must try to understand their strengths and, from this, the behaviours they are less comfortable enacting. If their failure to perform is because their role does not suit their behavioural strengths, then we should be working on how to:

- either re-position them to a role where their strengths will help them succeed or

- try to adjust the way in which they undertake it so it fits them more comfortably.

Such solutions will be good for them and good for the organisation.

This has profound implications for such activities as recruitment, promotions and also internal transfers.

You may recall the statistics I presented on morale/engagement in the Introduction:

- Only 5% are really enjoying themselves.

- 24% are comfortable.

- 34% don't feel particularly good.

- 37% are potentially fed up and looking to quit.

I have found the two of the most significant contributors to this are:

- Being in a role to which they are not behaviourally suited.

- Being managed in a way that is contrary to their nature. (e.g. The manager, rather than the role itself, puts time pressures on a patient and steady person.)

The ability to understand people is more effective if we have the objectivity of psychometrics to assist us in preventing inadvertent misplacement and/or mismanagement of them. However, without these tools, we must nevertheless make the effort to understand their behavioural strengths and limitations.

## *And if, despite all this, the individual is still underperforming?*

Then we have no option but to have a frank discussion — in an "Ask! Don't tell!" manner — about where we go from here. Maybe they have ambitions in a different kind of role in a different type of organisation, in which case we can facilitate their departure in a humane and helpful way.

If they are reasonable, they will be likely to appreciate the cooperation. On the other hand, if they are difficult (e.g. totally immature about it), then we do have recourse to all the documentation on their lack of progress and can honestly write our appraisal report accordingly.

We may even have to go so far as to seek inputs from Personnel/HR on the appropriate process for disciplinary action/dismissal.

# PART 3. Summary, Conclusion and Bibliography.

## 3.1. Summary.

*To Lead To Win and Pioneer Powerful Performance ...*

1. First, we need to know where we want to go, aligning our area with the company direction.

- Create a vision for our area encompassing "why we are here".

- Aim at delighting all our stakeholders (e.g. customers, owners, employees, etc.) in equal measure.

- Create focus on the key elements that support this:
  - ➢ Budget & Cost Control
  - ➢ Controls
  - ➢ Quality of our products/services
  - ➢ Revenue generation
  - ➢ Staff Morale
  - ➢ Timeliness of product/service delivery.

2. Now we need to create a positive environment that helps each team member be the best they can be and achieve great things. In so doing, we also assist them in getting where they want to go. We must therefore establish the tools and techniques that help make them successful.

Forget about theories of motivation and leadership. Instead focus on the objective and practical, which include the following points.

- Use the power of "Leading from Behind" to coach each individual, growing their ability to successfully "Score Sixes".

- Support this approach by adopting the discipline of "Ask! Don't tell!" that enhances true communication, builds rapport as well as planning and problem-solving ability.

- Guide them in using a practical approach to Action Planning, involving prioritisation, problem-solving, creativity/innovation, goal-setting and self-monitoring.

- Help them learn how to analyse situations to "prospect" for problems and opportunities, creating continuous improvement in performance.

- Ensure they hone and stretch their skills and abilities.

- Ensure their achievements are recorded with qualitative/quantitative measurements in respect of the six key areas. This leads to making Performance Appraisals motivational, as well as objective, simple and fair.


3. Remember: a company may claim they are doing most of this — but the real question is HOW they are doing it. The "HOW" is the vital, the critical, component that determines whether or not the result is Powerful Performance.

## 3.2. Conclusion.

This book has presented you with a practical way forward for significantly improving morale, engagement and performance. You can relatively quickly and easily learn from this what it has taken me years to discover and test.

I recommend you not only try this but adapt and improve on it. Develop it in a way that suits you and your team. Make it your own — and achieve powerful performance.

The potential is there, waiting to be unleashed. Harness it. Don't waste it!

I wish you every success.

# 3.3. Bibliography/Recommended Reading.

David L. Bradford & Allan R. Cohen: "Managing for Excellence". John Wiley & Sons (1984) ISBN: 0471871761

Patrick C. Connor: "Dimensions in Modern Management". Houghton Mifflin (1974) ISBN: 0395177413

Stephen R. Covey: "The 7 Habits of Highly Effective People". Simon & Schuster Ltd, ISBN-13: 978-0684858395

Finkelstein, Harvey & Lawton: "Breakout Strategy — Meeting The Challenge of Double-Digit Growth". McGraw Hill, 2007. ISBN - 0-07-145231-1

Daniel Goleman: "Emotional Intelligence: Why it can matter more than IQ". Bloomsbury Publishing (1995) ISBN: 0747526222

John P. Kotter, James L. Heskett: "Corporate Culture and Performance": The Free Press (1992) ISBN: 0029184673

Douglas McGregor: "The Human Side of Enterprise". McGraw-Hill (1960)

Douglas McGregor: "The Professional Manager". McGraw-Hill (1967)

Kerry Patterson, Joseph Grenny, Al Switzler, Ron McMillan: "The Balancing Act : Mastering the Competing Demands of Leadership". Thompson Executive Press (1996)   ISBN: 0967597501

For Notes & References for Action.

# About The Author — And His Other Books

Nigel J. Copsey has decades of experience in managing, training, consulting and coaching in a number of countries and even in unusual situations that presented some "interesting challenges."

From his relatively early years, he developed a passion: people, performance and productivity. This has remained with him and grown ever since.

During his career he has focused strongly upon performance improvement, rarely accepting the status quo. This resulted in a great deal of study, observation and experiment that, together with the many mistakes he made, taught him a great deal. In this book, he shares some of his learning.

More Books by Nigel J. Copsey.

*Non-Fiction - Management.*

**Lead To Win — Pioneering Powerful Performance.** (Leadership)
Available as both e-book and paperback

*Currently "Under Construction"...*

**The Pyramid Factor.** (A management parody in short story form.)

*Fiction.*

**Penny Wise — Spy Foolish.** (Humour)
**Short Tales From The East.** (Humour, General)

www.ingramcontent.com/pod-product-compliance
Lightning Source LLC
Chambersburg PA
CBHW051504170526
45166CB00001B/385